M000221509

JEDEDIAH
DAYS

JEDEDIAH DAYS

One Woman's Island Paradise

MARY PALMER

HARBOUR PUBLISHING

Harbour Publishing
P.O. Box 219
Madeira Park, BC V0N 2H0

Cover design, page design and composition by Martin Nichols, Lionheart Graphics
Cover photograph by Donald E. Waite, Waite Air Photos Inc., Maple Ridge, BC
Map by Hilary Stewart
All photographs from private family collections
unless credited otherwise.

Published with the assistance of The Canada Council and the Province of British Columbia through the British Columbia Arts Council.

Printed and bound in Canada.

Canadian Cataloguing in Publication Data

Palmer, Mary, 1920-
    Jedediah days

    ISBN 1-55017-184-4

    1. Palmer, Mary, 1920 2. Jedediah Island (B.C.)—Biography.
    3. Farm life—British Columbia—Jedediah Island.   4. Jedediah
    Island (B.C.)—History. I. Title.

FC3845.J42Z49 1998   971.1'31   C98-910226-2
F1089.J42P34 1998

THE CANADA COUNCIL | LE CONSEIL DES ARTS
FOR THE ARTS | DU CANADA
SINCE 1957 | DEPUIS 1957

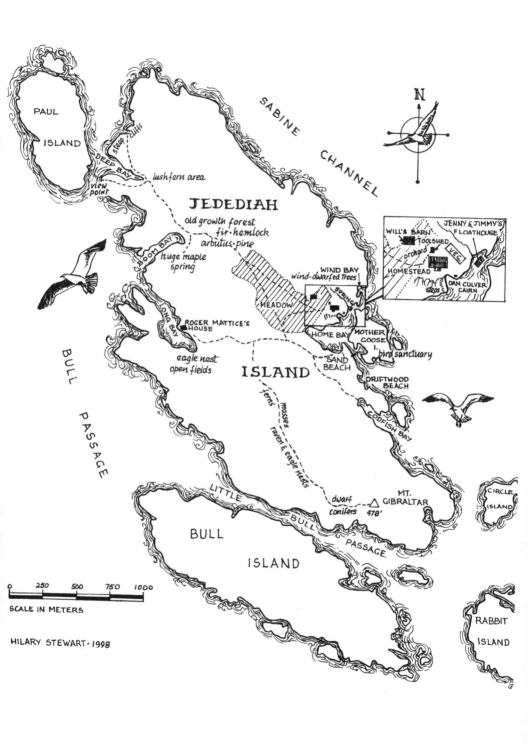

PAUL
ISLAND

SABINE CHANNEL

N

STEEP CLIFFS

DEEP BAY

lush fern area

view point

JEDEDIAH

old growth forest
fir · hemlock
arbutus · pine

BOOM BAY

huge maple
spring

LONG BAY

ROGER MATTICE'S
HOUSE

eagle nest
open fields

MEADOW

WIND BAY
wind-dwarfed trees

SPRING

HOME BAY

MOTHER
GOOSE
I.

bird sanctuary

SAND
BEACH

DRIFTWOOD
BEACH

ISLAND

ferns

mosses

raven & eagle nests

CODFISH BAY

BULL PASSAGE

WILL'S BARN
TOOLSHED

JENNY & JIMMY'S
FLOATHOUSE

orchard

HOMESTEAD

V.E.G.

steps

DAN CULVER
CAIRN

LITTLE

BULL

dwarf
conifers

MT.
GIBRALTAR
△
478'

CIRCLE
ISLAND

BULL

ISLAND

PASSAGE

0   250   500   750   1000

SCALE IN METERS

HILARY STEWART · 1998

RABBIT
ISLAND

Foreword

My introduction to Jedediah Island came through a telephone call from Pauline Tranfield. She told me that Mary and Al Palmer, owners of Jedediah Island, were interested in having their property dedicated as parkland, but their efforts to this end were being frustrated. Could I help?

From this point, to the happy announcement that agreement had been reached between the Province of British Columbia and Mary and Al Palmer for the formal establishment of Jedediah Island Provincial Marine Park, is indeed a long story. There were many helpful signs, false hopes and disappointing setbacks, but thanks to the combined efforts of many people and organizations, the Palmers' wish finally came true. To have played a part in this accomplishment provides considerable satisfaction and internal "warmth" to everyone who made a contribution, large or small. We can all share and rejoice in the success.

We do not know when Jedediah first emerged as an identifiable entity. Some 12,000 years ago, the great river of ice that flowed southward into the Pacific Ocean via Juan de Fuca Strait left exposed the topography we see today. The first aboriginal peoples may have arrived about this time, but evidence of their habitation on Jedediah is much more recent. These First Nations peoples kept their culture orally, so little is known about the early use of and impact on the island's resources.

When Archibald Menzies, surgeon and botanist on Captain George Vancouver's 1792 expedition, sailed through what we now know as the Strait of Georgia, he described these lands as vast stretches of pinery. His "pines" were in fact mostly Douglas firs (later named *Pseudotsuga menziezii* in his honour), and the extensive tall forests that so impressed him remain today only as small and isolated stands. On Jedediah, however, a large number of these stately trees from Menzies' time remain.

Jedediah has a second possible link with the earliest era of European exploration on the coast. Commanders Galiano and Valdes, Spanish explorers of the inside passage, may have released the ancestors of the wild goats that now roam the island. If this is true, the Spaniards were the first white people to set foot on Jedediah.

Sandwiched between Lasqueti and Texada islands, and "out of sight" of modern travel corridors, Jedediah then became the quiet domain of nineteenth-century homesteaders, and finally the home of Mary and Al Palmer.

In the BC government's quest to identify a provincial network that encompasses every representative landscape and bio-geoclimatic type, the inclusion of *all* Jedediah is very meaningful. Some alteration of the landscape has occurred, but large portions remain essentially untouched. Visitors to Jedediah can still experience some of the grandeur of the coastal Douglas fir forest that inspired Archibald Menzies more than two centuries ago.

To better appreciate and understand the latest chapter in Jedediah's long history, we must thank Mary Palmer for her diligence, and acknowledge all those who have visited and assisted her in pulling together the recollections of a special time and place. With *Jedediah Days* in hand, visitors to this provincial park can share some of the challenges and joys experienced by the Palmers, who truly made the island their home, and who decided to share their love of Jedediah with the rest of the world.

Bill Merilees
Nanaimo, BC
March 1998

Chapter

1

WORLD WAR II WAS OVER. NEW CHALLENGES WERE on the horizon. My husband Ed and I decided it was time to set sail among the many islands of Puget Sound and the coastal waters of British Columbia, in search of an idyllic setting to enhance our lifestyle.

Unexpectedly, our search ended with the publication of a real estate advertisement in a Seattle newspaper. The ad read: "Island for Sale, 640 acres in the Strait of Georgia, BC, Canada, write Box 475."

We promptly answered the ad, and a few evenings later the telephone rang. A crisp voice announced, "I am Mr. Shaw, the owner of Jedediah Island."

After a pause my husband answered, "Good evening Mr. Shaw. We are interested in your island in BC. Could you give us more information?"

"Sure, I'd be glad to, but I have a better idea. Why don't you make a trip up there and look it over for yourself? I'll arrange for a float plane to take you if you are certain you are seriously interested in the property."

"Yes, we are very interested," Ed replied.

"Could you be ready to go by this weekend?"

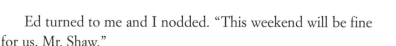

Ed turned to me and I nodded. "This weekend will be fine for us, Mr. Shaw."

"OK, I'll make the arrangements and get back to you."

Arrangements were made, and on a promising May morning in 1949 our chartered float plane took off from Kenmore near Seattle, Washington, for Jedediah Island, British Columbia. Humming high over the San Juan Islands of Washington state, we admired the sparkling mosaic of small isles nestled among grand stretches of larger, mountainous islands.

Suddenly, the coast became precipitous on the eastern horizon. A tremendously steep and rugged island arose. "That must be Texada Island," Ed shouted over the drone of the engines, "and the smaller one to the west Lasqueti."

The pilot nodded and replied, "I have flown over this part of BC before but never tried to land. Jedediah has to be the island right ahead of us between Texada and Lasqueti." The charts showed several reefs in the southern entrance to the island, so the pilot said he planned to circle the area, then come down outside the bay and taxi in.

As the pilot searched for a safe landing, the plane seemed to touch the tops of the tall evergreens. Below us, green patches of clearings were dotted with grazing animals. At the end of the largest clearing, several ramshackle buildings leaned into the landscape. The shimmering water seemed to leap up at us. "Steady now," the pilot yelled, "I'm bringing her down." Holding white-knuckled to the back of the forward seat, I was ready. The plane's pontoons thumped, bumped and touched down, and we glided in between the reefs. The pilot cut the motor, jumped out of the plane and tied a rope from the plane to a beached log. Ed bailed out of the cockpit onto a log and I followed. We untied the plane and the pilot assured us he would be back for us tomorrow, at high tide, around four in the afternoon.

My first husband Ed Mattice and I with our sons Evan and Roger, 1949. That year we decided to buy Jedediah Island.

Seaweed strewn among the slippery rocks made the ascent to the path above a challenge. As the rocks moved under our hiking boots, tiny pugnacious crabs confronted us boldly, waving their front claws.

On a knoll above the beach rose an ancient house. Its frame was perched on tall stilts of beach logs. Under the peak of the roof, a second storey jutted out as if preparing to be taken off with the next gale. Gaping holes in the roof gave birds easy access. Long, narrow empty windows framed sunken black holes. Leaning out to sea, the tired structure seemed ready to give up the ghost. Two ancient gnarled lilac shrubs with festoons of mauve blossoms stood side by side near the doorway, like sentinels. Under the eaves a warped wooden barrel rested. Ed leaned over its edge and pulled out a desiccated corpse which possibly had been a raccoon. I screeched, "Drop that thing, and let's go inside."

We were welcomed inside by a flurry of wings. Irritated by our intrusion, swallows dove down to our heads on their way up to the high beams of the ceiling. Cup-shaped nests made of mud, feathers, bits of grass and twigs were cemented tightly to the beams. The walls of the room were blackened with ages of soot from the fireplace, stove and kerosene lanterns. Rusting away against a brick chimney, a monstrous wood cooking stove was on its last legs. On the other side of the chimney stood a small English fireplace. Its face was decorated with pebbles, shells and multicoloured pieces of glass. I gazed out of the bare windows onto a sparkling view of the bay.

Opening into the parlour were two small bedrooms, divided by a small staircase. Upstairs, three more bedrooms joined a hallway. Tall open windows offered spectacular views.

"Oh look, there's Texada," I said. "It's a couple of miles from us, but it seems that I can reach out and touch it." Its towering mountain peak reached to the sky and tumbled to sea. The fjord-like channel between us and Texada teemed with tugs, fish boats and windblown sailboats.

We went back downstairs and outdoors, where a grassy path led us to an ancient orchard. In perfect formation, rows of apple, pear, cherry, plum and nut trees stood decorated with clusters of pink and white blossoms. We counted eighty-four trees in all. "Ed, see how the tree branches grow high up from the main stock," I said. He replied that deer and other animals were probably reaching up and pruning off the lower branches, maintaining a high crown in the tree. We rambled along into a long, narrow wood-planked barn. Inside, parts of well-worn farming equipment rested on the dirt floor. Harnesses and other animal trappings were draped over rough railings. Picking up part of a horse collar, I rubbed the worn leather with my thumb, feeling the smooth texture of the hide. Rusty horseshoes hung on thick, square-headed nails.

We passed through the barn's double doors, into an open clearing ringed by undulating hills that rose to heights of three hundred feet, then sloped gently down toward the clearing. Grazing in the open fields were flocks of sheep with long, straggly tails and thick woolly coats.

Turning toward me and taking my hand in his, Ed looked

directly at me. "Mary, this place is far too isolated, too distant from civilization," he said. "The buildings are almost beyond repair. In a word, it's overwhelming." I looked away, gazing at the surrounding hills with a feeling of strong affinity to this land, and a rush of déjà vu. As we started back to the house, we heard a rustling, and out of a thicket popped a roly-poly chap. He walked toward us, reaching down and pulling out one of his heavy socks that had worked down into his gumboots. Striped suspenders plus a wide leather belt gave support to his tweedy brown wool fisherman's pants. As he came closer, we could see a fringe of white curly hair twisted around the edges of a home-knit wool cap.

He spoke first, in a thick Scottish brogue. "I'm Jimmy Riddell, folks around here call me a riddle. I bet you're the Yankee folks from Seattle that might be figuring to buy Jedediah. We just got a letter from Mr. Shaw saying that you may be looking the place over soon. Mail here is usually mighty slow and not too important to us. It often depends if you want to fish along the way and the weather is obliging for rowing a boat a couple of miles over to Lasqueti to pick it up. We were out of fish, and the weather was calm, so I ventured over to check on the news of the world. Now that you are here, what do you think of the rock?"

"What we've seen so far is spectacular," Ed answered, "but overwhelming."

"Guess you haven't had a chance to look over much of the place yet," Jimmy said. "Wait until you see the sheep and goats that roam the hills. I've been chasing one of the sheep for a couple of hours to get within shooting range, but no luck yet. Then I saw you folks down on the flats." I ventured forward to extend my hand; Jimmy grasped it firmly and I realized his first two fingers were missing. "I lost my fingers cleaning fish on my boat, the *Quit*, years ago," he explained.

Ed shook hands too, introducing us as Mary and Ed Mattice.

"Would you like to follow me to our float house and meet Mrs. Hughes, a former longtime owner of Jedediah?" Jimmy asked us.

"Very much," was Ed's reply.

"All right, come along while I go back up the trail for my gun. I left it by a tree when I noticed you."

We followed Jimmy along the edge of the clearing and down a narrow ravine, where his gun leaned against a huge fir tree. He threw the gun over his shoulder and we continued to a small stream. "This is where our water comes from," Jimmy told us. "It never runs dry, as it's fed by an underground spring." We followed the stream down and reached an open bay. Carefully we made our way along two thick planks attached to an anchored driftwood float. A tiny dwelling clung to the end of the float, perched there as though it had been washed up after a fierce storm. All sorts of flotsam and jetsam was tied or nailed to its shaky frame.

"Jenny, we have company!" Jimmy shouted.

Hesitantly, a tall, thin lady stepped out of the doorway. Her thin wisps of grey-brown hair were fastened tightly into a bun at the nape of her long neck. Her soft blue eyes looked directly into mine as she spoke. "How do you do, I am Mrs. Hughes," she said. "Would you kindly like to join Jimmy and me in a cup of tea?"

"We would really enjoy that, after our hike," I answered. As soon as we had walked through a small doorway, we were surrounded by strange and wonderful treasures. A shiny brass kettle danced and hissed on the black iron stove. Jenny poured hot water into a brown betty teapot. My eyes widened at the sight of an odd table in the centre of the room. It was shaped like a bass fiddle, only narrower, and the wood was highly polished. Three stout hand-hewn legs supported the table. "Don't be alarmed," Jimmy smiled. "It's only a coffin that I made into a table. You'd be surprised by all the strange paraphernalia that washes ashore in a southeast storm. The inside of this coffin was lined with satin. Jenny fashioned it into blouses, shirts and pillow covers."

He went on to tell us about the freighter *Courtenay Transfer* that travels between Vancouver and Courtenay, passing Jedediah in the Sabine Channel. Often in winter storms her tow of barges broke up and goods washed ashore. "Last year we found a chest of drawers full of clothes ready to wear," Jimmy said. "One depression winter, sides of bacon, sacks of onions and potatoes and other goodies filled our cupboards. Look at the boards on the floor. They are painted with paint we picked up on the beach, and the *Quit* is always colourful with 'breakup' paint. Maybe you noticed the piles of lumber above the high tide mark. It's from breakups of ships like the *Courtenay Transfer*. It gives us a 'Ma Perkins' lumberyard at our beck and call."

Home Bay, Jedediah Island, at low tide. Lucky for us, oysters found this beach a great place to live.

"Do you think you'll be able to adapt to island living?" Jenny asked, as she offered us Scottish shortbread.

I was unprepared for the question. "I think I can," I said slowly. "I spent my youth in the mountains of the Olympic Peninsula in Washington state, just across the Juan de Fuca Strait. My stepfather was an independent 'gyppo' logger. We lived in tents with sides and roofs of cedar slabs, and we had outdoor plumbing and got our water from a creek. My friends were the animals of the forest. My mother and I moved to the city when I was sixteen, to avoid the possibility of meeting my true love among the virgin timber. In the city, I met and fell in love with this fellow by my side."

As I spoke, Jenny had been nervously folding the pleats in her dark grey skirt. Looking down, she asked Ed, "What do you think of this island?"

Ed began awkwardly. "You see, I'm a city fellow, and all of this overwhelms me. It's so idyllic, yet so isolated and rugged." Then he turned to me. "I'm not sure the many adjustments I'd have to make to live here would suit my present lifestyle."

Jenny refilled our cups and passed us more shortbread, as Jimmy said, "Jenny is a fine cook and gardener. The only drawback to our cozy life is that she makes me sleep on the *Quit* until Canon Greene comes by on one of his mission ship visits, to make us man and wife. Anyway, I won't marry her until she's sixty-five, and gets her old age pension—which is next month. A fellow can't live in high style on only one pension."

Jenny's cheeks darkened to a deep red. "Jimmy Riddell, you are impossible!" she said.

"Jenny, may I ask you how you found Jedediah?" I asked.

"Yes," she replied, "it was a long time ago when I fell in love with Jedediah and met and married Mr. Hughes. It was 1932 and I had just immigrated from England, settled in Vancouver, and found a job nursing at St. Paul's Hospital. On a holiday with some sailing friends, we dropped anchor in one of the bays here and went ashore to stretch our legs. On the trail, we encountered a wiry middle-aged man who introduced himself as Henry Hughes, accompanied by a large black dog. He invited us into his house, which was at that time lovely, well kept and comfortable. He was a graduate of Trinity College, Dublin, and had immigrated from Ireland. He planned to raise sheep on Jedediah, and brought along to the island with him a manservant, cook, gardener and shepherd. Unfortunately, he was not a practical man. His once-substantial resources dwindled, his help left the island, and finally only he, his faithful dog and his fine sheep remained."

Jenny walked over to a drawer, pulled out a letter and held it out to Ed. "This is a letter written by a good friend, a tugboat captain. It gives an interesting account of Mr. Hughes."

Jenny and Henry Hughes (at left) outside the house at Home Bay, with Jenny's sister Mrs. Kerr and her two children, 1930s. Jenny met Henry Hughes, owner of Jedediah, in 1932 when she and some friends stopped there on a sailing holiday. After Henry died, Jenny and Jimmy Riddell got together, and when I met her in 1949, she and Jimmy lived in a tiny float house anchored at Jedediah.

Ed began reading aloud from the letter, which was from a Mr. James Anderson.

I was very pleased and interested in hearing from you and so sorry of Mr. Hughes' passing. He was strictly from the academic world, not too suited to the rugged life of the coast. As you are probably aware, the owners prior to Mr. Hughes had several tragedies that made it difficult to continue living on Jedediah. In a chat with Mr. Hughes after I gained his confidence, I gathered that he expected to resell the island to the CPR, who in turn would develop it as a summer resort to compete with Bowen Island, which was then controlled by the Union Steamship Company which had developed the Union Estates on the Island. However, the CPR bought Newcastle Island instead, close to Nanaimo. It did some development, but the great depression of the 30s put an end to the project.

Ed took a sip of tea and continued.

When we would be steaming past Jedediah, before I actually met Mr. Hughes, I scanned the property with binoculars and occasionally I would catch a glimpse of this bearded man and his black dog. I'd heard stories about him from some of the Lasqueti folks—apparently there were disagreements about a school tax. He had no children, and there were neither schools nor roads on Jedediah to justify paying taxes, in his view. To make matters worse, he went to a family home on Lasqueti for a Sunday dinner and became quite upset when his dog companion, Caesar, had to eat outdoors with the rest of the canines, because there wasn't a place set for him at the table.

Our tug the *Active* had been tied up to Paul Island for a week to wait out a storm, when I decided to stretch my legs on Jedediah and hike the trails. As I remember, one trail goes from the cove through a draw with a steep rock on the left. As you come out past the rock it opens into a large meadow. There was a drainage ditch along the western boundary of the meadow and inside the meadow next to the ditch was a stretch of snake fence. I jumped the ditch and was about to climb over the fence, when Mr. Hughes stood up out of the tall grass with what looked like a 303, pointing in the general direction of my navel and in a quiet, firm voice said, "This is as far as you go young man, turn right around and leave my land." My first impression was that I had met a real bushed hermit who was right over the edge, then I quickly realized that his eyes were very sane appearing and he seemed very controlled, he just didn't want company, certainly not strangers. I apologized and explained that I was off a ship and was just out for a walk. He said, "You are trespassing on private property, I do not encourage trespassing."

As I headed back up the trail, I thought, I'm going to make a friend of that man if it's the last thing I do. It was about a month later, we were tied up to a log boom next to Jedediah, when I had an opportunity to try my luck again. This time I had some ammunition. I took some late issues of the *Vancouver Sun* and *Province* and a roll of London *Daily Mirror*s, which I got from an English stoker we had aboard the tug. Folks had told me if he'd spend more time working his place and less time reading he would be better off, so I knew I had the right ammunition.

Sure enough, he stopped me exactly as before, reminding me that I had been told of his desire for privacy. I assured him that I hadn't forgotten, I was coming to ask permission to go on a hike, but if he said no, I would head back to the ship immediately.

But in the meantime I wanted to drop off the newspapers that we had finished with. He accepted the newspapers but didn't encourage further conversation, so I headed back up the trail. This procedure went on for some time, except after the third time, he would meet me without the gun and we'd have a little conversation. I'm of the opinion he felt some boat's crews or fishermen had poached some of his sheep.

One afternoon several weeks later, I walked over and got quite a start—he wasn't at the fence, in fact he was nowhere in sight. I immediately thought he had come to some sort of harm. But smoke was coming out of the chimney so I knew he was alive. The dog Caesar came to meet me before I got to the house. In fact Caesar and I were quite good friends by this time. I used to bring him goodies from the ship when I brought the newspapers for Mr. Hughes. Mr. Hughes was splitting wood when I approached. I invited him and Caesar back to the ship for supper. I had carefully timed the invitation. On the *Active* the officers ate separately from the crew. I timed it so we would get there just as the skipper and two engineers were finished. In this way Caesar could be treated like an honoured guest. A place was set for him on the settee next to Mr. Hughes and he ate with us. Mr. Hughes had the time of his life and I finally could say we were friends. I will miss him very much when we steam by Jedediah.

Best wishes,
Jim Anderson

Ed handed the letter to Jenny and she carefully placed it back in the drawer. "Thank you so much, Jenny," said Ed, "for a glimpse of the past. We'd best take our leave and see a bit more of Jedediah before dark." We expressed our appreciation for their warm welcome and sharing tea and memories with us. Then we hastily stepped along the entrance planks to steady ground and headed up to the old house.

"We'd better straighten out our sleeping bags and put our food in order," Ed offered. "It will be dark soon."

"How about hiking to the top of that hill when we come back," I suggested. "It looks like the highest part of the island."

Following a sheep and goat trail, we started up a slight mound. Our boots sunk softly into spongy moss almost to our ankles. "Step along as quietly as possible, Mary," Ed said. "We might be lucky and find deer, goats, sheep or other animals." Down the other side of the mound, we found ourselves deep in underbrush of salal, ferns and huckleberry. Overhead were red limbs of arbutus. Giant fir, spruce and pine limbs reached to the sky. As we climbed higher the underbrush became straggly and scarce. A few lone pines struggled against the wind. In a small clearing a shallow pool of water was being visited by a group of six or seven sleek brown and black goats, with long, twisted sabrelike horns that bent directly back from the tops of their heads. A light breeze blew away from us. We froze silently to watch them, but after a few seconds the lookout goat uttered a loud snort and they all were alerted. They stood and stared at us before bolting away into a ravine below. "Weren't they magnificent?" Ed laughed. "They would be great to have around if their stench wasn't so strong!" We continued to climb and soon reached the summit called Gibraltar by the locals. Only mosses, lichens and scrubby pines covered the landscape at the top. "Look there's Mount Baker. Mary, we really aren't so far away

Young homesteaders hiking on Jedediah, c. 1913. Left to right:
"Olive," "Carey," Oscar Olmstead, Winnie Jelly, Myrtle (Foote)
King. The child just visible at front is Harry or Dorothy Olmstead.

Morris Jelly on his homestead, 1915.

from home." The mountain and sea glistened in the late afternoon sunlight. The silence was startling.

Near us stood a cairn with a glass jar resting in the centre of the pile of stones. Inside the jar was a small notebook and pencil. Many names and dates covered the yellowed paper. "Alma Olmstead, Harry Olmstead, Dorothy Olmstead, July 2, 1912. Thelma Jelly, Mervyn Jelly, August 3, 1916, N. Washburn. Mary Foote, Lester Foote, Morris Jelly, 1914" were a few of the names, along with Jimmy Riddell, Henry Hughes and Jim Anderson. Ed added our names to the list. We watched two eagles perched on the topmost dead branch of a pine. When they left the branch they spun and soared downward, diving gracefully in search of prey. "Mary, we'd best be getting back," Ed said as the sunlight faded.

"Hold up for me," I screeched, as we tumbled down the side of the hill, rolling along and sliding on loose rocks and slippery mosses.

"Better hurry up if we are going to see any more of the island before dark!" Ed yelled.

We scuttled down the steep terrain, low-growing blackberry vines catching our ankles and tangling and tripping our steps. Thick salal and young arbutus branches slapped us in the face as we struggled toward the open meadow.

Ed asked me whether I felt up to hiking to the north reach of the island to check out a safe boat moorage, and I said, "I'm with you." Following a skid road of split cedar, we walked among gigantic fir, spruce and cedar trees, with alder and arbutus reaching to the sunlight through the evergreens. A few huge stumps were scattered about. I traced my fingers through an undercut on a huge fir that someone had started to fell, but for some reason had left to grow. "Can you believe the hardships and struggles these fellows experienced cutting this timber and getting it to the water?" I said to Ed. Modern equipment like chain saws and power skidders wasn't available then. They had probably used steam donkeys and horses or oxen to drag the logs to the water, as my stepdad had done in the 1920s and '30s. The trail led downward to a long, narrow deep-water cove. A tugboat was attached to the shore by a steel wire cable, and two sailboats and a powerboat were anchored in the cove. The chatter of the boat people was drowned out by the clamour of the seabirds above. A lanky, tanned fellow from one of the sailboats shouted, "Bon soir!" We waved back.

We returned to the trail as the sun dropped quickly. By the time we reached the house, the darkness was deep and the quiet was deafening. We quickly succumbed to sleep.

Cracks in the walls and open windows let in the dawn the next morning. Footsteps up the path and a shout of "Top of the morning to you" was the first thing we heard. "Jenny has steaming bowls of thick Scotch oatmeal, toasted homemade bread and tea ready for you!" Jimmy called.

"Thanks, Jimmy, we'll be right down," we answered. We

Home Bay at twilight.

shook ourselves, stretched, jumped into our outer clothing and shoes, and splashed our faces outside in a pitted granite wash basin. Down the path we went, over the planks and into the float house. Inside the air was filled with the latest and most popular soap opera of the day, "Ma Perkins." The chatter came from a high shelf in a far corner of the room, where there was a radio attached to a large car battery. Jenny jumped over and turned it off. "Jimmy," she sputtered, "you can't play that thing all the time, the battery will run down and you'll have to charge it with the *Quit*'s generator again." Turning to us, she asked, "Did you sleep well?"

"We sure did," Ed answered. "All that hiking is not an everyday event in our lives back home." We placed ourselves around the coffin table. Steaming tea was poured from the brown betty and English stone bowls were heaped with oatmeal and covered with a dark brown sugar. I asked Jenny what it was.

"It's called Demerara sugar. I use it quite a bit in baking cakes and cookies," she replied. "Your powdered sugar is called icing sugar in

Jenny Hughes (right) and a friend, 1940.

England and Canada. A few words are different here from the States, and some spellings differ also." She turned over the homemade toast as it browned on top of the wood-fired cook stove. "Here, have some of my English orange marmalade on your toast. Jimmy, please pour more tea for everyone."

Jimmy poured a full round. "What do you think of the old rock?" he asked. "Have you decided on buying it?"

Ed looked at me before he answered. "Well, it's a bit far from Seattle, and it's going to take a fair amount of work and money to get the house livable and the barns and fences in order. Also we haven't come to a firm price or looked into the taxes and other costs. Right now I'd say it's questionable." I had to nod in agreement.

Jenny placed a small wood log in the firebox of the stove. "Mr. Hughes and I sold because we just couldn't pay the land taxes," she said. "Also we were getting too old to run a profitable herd of sheep and found it impossible to hire help. We sold to Mr. Shaw and moved to Pender Harbour. We became quite unhappy there and Mr. Hughes passed away soon after. Our good friend Jimmy came out to the island one day shortly after his death and has worked for Mr. Shaw ever since."

Mr. Shaw had intended to move to the island with his large family, Jenny told us. Too hastily he placed his family and his household belongings on a barge from Vancouver to the island. It was October and a fierce southeast gale battered the barge almost to bits. "The captain of the tug turned around and returned to Vancouver, and we haven't seen Mr. Shaw since. Now that he is selling the island we are in a quandary."

"Jenny and Jim," I responded, "Ed and I have talked over the problems and possibilities of the island. We agree we could not live on Jedediah permanently at this time. We have two young sons in school, and a business that needs our constant attention. But if we become the new owners you are more than welcome to live on the island as long as you like." Ed nodded in agreement.

Jenny beamed and replied, "That's a real comfort to know. We appreciate it very much."

Jimmy began to roll a cigarette. He held the thin tobacco

paper between his shaky fingers and poured a pinch of the tobacco out of the can into the paper. More tobacco spilled on his woolly pants and the floor than into the partly rolled paper. He wet the edges of the paper with his tongue as he rolled the cigarette. Then he struck a match on the stove and began to puff away. In between puffs he expressed his gratitude.

Ed extended his hand to Jimmy and Jenny. "You both have made our trip here most enjoyable, thank you kindly," he said.

I gave both of our new friends a big hug and farewell. "Hope to see you both again soon," I said. "Keep the lantern in the window for us."

Ed spoke first as we made our way to the empty house. "Mary, you shouldn't have given them too much hope. They are a gentle, trusting couple."

"Yes, I know, but it just seemed right to say."

Ed shrugged and said, "I think I hear the float plane."

On our return, we were too quickly into the rhythm of city life, the island far behind us. One hot, dry afternoon, as I was tending to some of our nursery stock, a fellow walked up to me and said, "I understand that this spring you made a trip to British Columbia, to look into buying an island."

"Yes," I replied.

"In spring and summer I go up to Campbell River on Vancouver Island to fish for the big ones," he said, "and I heard the island you were interested in was sold."

"Oh no!" I exclaimed.

As the fellow bent down to select a small flowering azalea from the nursery, Ed came by and said that Mr. Shaw, the owner of Jedediah, was on the telephone. I picked up the phone and greeted him.

"I just finished talking to your husband," Mr. Shaw said, "and he told me you folks had a wonderful trip to Jedediah, but felt the island wasn't for you."

"It's a coincidence you called when you did. We were just discussing the island with a fellow here and he said he heard a rumour that the island was sold."

"Not to my knowledge," said Mr. Shaw. "Did you have an opportunity to see Mrs. Hughes and Jimmy Riddell?"

"Oh yes, they made our visit very pleasant and interesting," I replied.

"Did they tell you about my near move to Jedediah?"

"Yes, they told us a bit."

"Well," he said slowly, "we bought the island, for more than I am asking now, from Mr. and Mrs. Hughes. We packed up too quickly, lock, stock and barrel, and placed it all on a scow. Including my mother-in-law. A tug from Vancouver towed us and the scow to the south entrance of Home Bay on Jedediah. It was late October and a strong southeast wind began to howl. The tugboat captain hauled the scow around to the north of the island and we anchored in a deep cove that was well protected from the storm. There we waited for several days for the wind to cease, and each day the tug company added several hundred dollars to its charges.

"Finally the captain pulled anchor and towed the scow back to Vancouver. All our·belongings were then reloaded onto trucks and taken back to Seattle. The entire family was discouraged and I put the island up for sale at once. My mother-in-law is most happy."

"Is your selling price firm, Mr. Shaw?"

"Yes, Mrs. Mattice, it is. I have lost so much in the transaction in time and money, and I know the island is worth a great deal more than what I am asking for it."

"All right, Mr. Shaw, we'll seriously talk about it and call you back in a few days."

Ed and I had many spirited discussions in the days that followed. The island was located too far from Seattle for weekend jaunts and the house and buildings were in need of major repairs. The island would be more suitable for a future retirement residence. It could only be used now as a summer retreat for us and the boys during school holidays.

Finally we called Mr. Shaw, arranged to meet him and came to an agreement on price and other terms. The deal was struck. We were now proud owners of Jedediah Island.

Later we learned that Jedediah was named for Jedediah S. Tucker, whose brother served with Admiral Earl St. Vincent of the British Navy. Jedediah wrote a biography of Admiral St. Vincent in 1844.

Now that Ed and I had closed the deal with Mr. Shaw, we began to get our boat, the *PBY*, ready for a trip to Jedediah for the summer holidays. The *PBY* had been converted from the hull of an amphibian flying boat that had served as an air–sea rescue plane during World War II. To look at her sleek lines, you'd think she was a speed queen, but her Chrysler marine engine barely allowed her to plough through the water at 6 to 8 knots. Not a very practical vessel!

The day school was finished, we were ready to return to Jedediah for the summer holidays. Our sons Evan and Roger were ecstatic. They had been gathering their gear for ages. Camping equipment, food and other supplies were loaded and stored aboard the *PBY*. Presuming all was shipshape, we left our moorage just before dawn to avoid any crowding at the Hiram Chittendom locks in Ballard. Ed navigated the vessel well through the locks and we entered the open waters of Puget Sound. The morning was glorious, we were on our way to Shangri-La and everyone was anticipating an exciting adventure—when the *PBY*'s motor gave a sputter, groaned and died. Ed was at a loss. He tried to get it started again but to no avail.

Near us a fellow mariner waved and yelled, "Need any help?"

Ed shouted back, "We sure do!"

"Throw me a rope and tie the other end to your bow," called the rescuer. We were grateful to get a tow to the Everett yacht basin.

"She seemed in great running order before we left," Ed sputtered. "I'd better stay here and get it repaired before we take off again and the same damn thing happens. You and the boys go ahead to the island and I'll join you when the boat is running right."

Four weary, disenchanted would-be adventurers crawled into their boat bunks and slept at dockside. In the morning I took a bus back to Seattle and drove our station wagon to the boat basin. We loaded our gear into the car, and the boys and I headed north.

"Mom, how are we going to get to the island in a station wagon?" Evan asked.

"Hey, fella," I answered, "we are going to find a boat or seaplane to take us."

They cheered up right away.

I had heard there were freight boats that transported supplies and people along the coast. Driving along the industrial waterfront of Vancouver, I inquired at several steamship companies and found a ship that was leaving in a few hours for stops up the coast, including Pender Harbour.

The clerk at the shipping office showed me a safe place on Gore Street to leave the station wagon while we were away, then the boys and I carried our equipment and supplies to the ship. The *Cardena* was a bit of a relic, but she had a passenger capacity of 250, she could carry 350 tons of freight, and she had a refrigerator compartment that would hold up to 30 tons of boxed fish. She served more than two hundred ports on the coast. Cannery workers, loggers, miners and tourists were grateful to sail with her.

Shouts of "Get aboard, we're ready to leave!" could be heard over the thunderous pounding of the ship's engines.

"Good God, lady, are you going on some kind of world expedition with all this gear?" said the crewman at the gangway. "Hey, kid, you can't bring that pea shooter aboard this ship."

"That's no pea shooter," Roger explained, "it's a .22 rifle and it's my dad's."

"Sorry," I interrupted, "but it's not loaded."

"OK, lady, but usually no guns are to be brought on the *Cardena*, it's the rules."

Ropes were released from the wharf. Grinding engines vibrated and jerked the vessel first forward and then in reverse. Whistles sounded and the boys squealed with delight, running from side to side and deck to deck in anticipation of the voyage. Stepping over a raised ledge in a doorway, I found myself in a small, low-ceilinged lounge with other upcoast travellers. Passengers were loitering about, some sitting on heavy wooden chairs and others standing at the large portholes watching the *Cardena* pass under the Lion's Gate Bridge. I found an empty chair next to a thirtyish woman.

"Do you know how long it will take to reach Pender Harbour?" I offered.

Turning her head slowly to me she answered, "No, this is my first trip up the coast. I'm heading for Powell River, to cook at a logging camp near there. I dunno much about this part of the country. Whatcha doing aboard?" She adjusted her brightly coloured kerchief under her chubby chin.

"Oh, I'm taking my boys to our summer place near Pender Harbour."

The woman became silent and held her thick, stubby hands close together in her lap, with her head down. Then she spoke quietly. "I just come over here to Canada from my home in Finland, and I am pretty lonesome for my people back home."

"Yes, you must be missing your old home and family very much," I responded with a pat on her shoulder. "But I know you'll soon make new friends and find a good life upcoast."

She glanced up at me with almost a smile.

Brawny, raw-boned men streamed through the doorway and settled down with their bottles of rye whisky. Cards were dealt. Cigars, pipes and Copenhagen snuffboxes were pulled out of mackinaw pockets. Soon swirls of smoke rose and the din of conversation filled the cramped, airtight room. The few women passengers began to leave.

My Finnish friend followed me out onto the open deck. "Whew," she exhaled, "it's better out here."

"Oh, much better," I echoed. "Excuse me. I'd best look and see what my two boys are up to."

Son Roger was giving unwanted instructions to his younger brother Evan on how to take photos. "Gosh, Mom, he doesn't even know how to focus a camera right," Roger complained. "He just runs around and snaps pictures."

"He's only five," I said. "But you could be helpful and patient with him."

All the while the most spectacular scenery rose before us. Snow-veiled mountains seemed to be tumbling down into the sea, and trees bent by the whims of the wind clung for life to the rocky blue-black coastline. Mighty tugboats pulled long floating log booms. Fishing boats with their poles extended and a few drifting sailboats added to the scene. Only a few dwellings lay scattered along the shoreline.

I had just found a secluded niche near the pilothouse to stretch out in the warm afternoon sun when suddenly I felt the ship slow down and make a sharp turn. The *Cardena*'s engines slowed and she steamed between two small islands into the narrow opening of a harbour. A scuffling was heard in the lounge. "Any of you boys getting off at Pender?" The door of the lounge opened with a thud and several fellows, some in rumpled expensive suits, others in rough work clothes, thrust themselves from the room.

"God, Harry, this time I'm going to make it back to camp with my caulk boots, last trip you cleaned me even to my boots."

"Oh, don't bitch to me about your goddamn rotten luck. It's very few times you haven't skunked us all in the deal." A swarthy, stocky chap went over to the ship's railing and with great gusto ejected a mouthful of half-chewed Copenhagen. Thanks to the leeward wind there was no fallout. He straightened up to his full height and bellowed, "OK, blokes, let's get off this tub!"

We disembarked with our gear and stood on the high wooden wharf in the wilderness. Where and how do we get from here to Jedediah? Glancing up from the dock, I noticed a two-storey rambling building with a long verandah reaching from one end to the other along the front. Above read a sign: Irvine's Landing, Rooms To Let.

"Come on, boys," I urged, "let's get up there and have a look."

On the top step of the verandah, a tall, lanky man, looking like dried beef with his weatherbeaten features, greeted us. "What can I do for you, lady?" I told him we needed a room for the night. He took us to a room at the end of a long, dark hallway. Our gear was stowed along one wall. A sign tacked on the faded wallpaper read: "Lights out at 10 o'clock, meals served promptly at 6, 12 and 6, only four people allowed in the dining room at one time, room with meals 5 dollars a day."

"Come on, fellows, it's nearly 6," I said to the boys. "You don't want to miss your first meal here." We tumbled down the stairs to the dining room and waited our turn. The boys were too excited about the great adventures before them to do justice to their meal, but the fare was wholesome and welcome.

Evan pulled at my hands and pleaded, "Come on, Mom, let's go down and look at the boats."

"OK," I nodded. "Maybe we can find someone to take us over to Jedediah."

We walked along the wharf and I asked a fellow working on a troller whether he would be interested in taking us and our gear over to Jedediah. "Sorry lady," he said, "but I have to get out to the fishing grounds early in the morning. You might ask that guy with the light green boat down at the end of the dock." I went to the light green boat and asked again, "Would you be willing to take me and my boys and our gear and supplies to Jedediah?"

"To where?" he inquired.

"To Jedediah Island. It's at the south end of Texada, between Texada and Lasqueti islands."

"Oh yeah. I know the place. Whatcha going over there for?"

"I'm taking my boys there for a summer holiday," I answered.

"Well, I guess it's a good place for that, but pretty isolated and rugged over there. When do you want to go over?"

"In the morning, but first I have to get more supplies."

"I'll take you over in the boat to Lloyd's store for supplies," he volunteered.

"First, how much do you charge for the trip?"

He twisted his wool hat and mumbled, "With the price of gas what it is and all, it'll be 25 bucks."

I agreed. "I'll see you at nine in the morning, ready to pick up supplies and go." He jumped back on his fish boat and disappeared below.

All the while, Evan had been leaning over the side of the dock watching small fish flashing and flitting in the water. "Gee, Roger, we could catch these easy," he boasted.

Roger ignored him. "Hey, Mom," he said, "let's get some

more fishing gear to really catch the big ones."

"We'll see," I replied. On the horizon a vermilion sunset blazed. "Come on, fellas, we'd better turn in. It'll be a big day tomorrow." As we stood on the hotel verandah, two blinks of the lights gave us a warning that in an hour the electric generator would be shut off for the night. The harbour overflowed with pleasure boats, fishing vessels, tugs, small runabouts and rowboats. In the summer of 1949, Pender Harbour was a hive of activity.

Upstairs I told the boys to go to the washroom before the lights went out. The single washroom at the end of the hall was shared by all the guests. I turned the round white porcelain doorknob and found inside a primitive bathtub with streaks of rust running down the centre. Huge black iron claws held the tub so high it was difficult to step over the side. A small white wash basin was fastened to the wall by the commode.

"Hey, Mom, what's this box over the toilet with a chain hanging down for?"

"Pull it and find out," was my answer.

He pulled. "Gosh, what a neat idea!" he squealed as the water drained from the tank into the bowl below.

"We'd better enjoy these facilities," I told them. "It's going to be a while before we'll have such luxury on the island."

We all three crept into a huge iron-railed bed with a mattress that kept us together in a snug heap in the centre, and slept until we heard banging on our door. In between the poundings, someone called, "Breakfast is ready, be down in ten minutes or it'll be too late."

"Yes, thank you, we'll be right down," I called back.

"Hey, where are my socks?" Roger moaned.

"Try looking under the bed. Come on, Evan, rise and shine."

After breakfast we gathered up our gear and checked out of

the inn. The boys and I tossed our supplies on board the fish boat, the skipper untied the lines and we putted over to Lloyd's Store for more supplies. As the boat approached the store dock, Roger jumped to the wharf and held the ropes ready to be fastened by the skipper.

We walked up the boat ramp and were met by a few old-timers sitting on a wooden bench soaking up the early morning sun and local goings-on.

"Top of the morning to you," one of them greeted us.

"Good morning to you all," I answered.

I lifted the heavy iron latch and the store doors opened slowly. Inside, counters, shelves, hooks and hangers from the ceiling beams were bending with every imaginable necessity for upcoast living. Searching up and down the aisles and overhead, we filled boxes and baskets with tinned butter, eggs preserved in silicone gel, canned milk and toilet paper. Flour, sugar, lard, salt, potatoes and other sundries were brought down to the dock and readied to be packed into the boat. Mr. Lloyd, the storekeeper, was most gracious and gave us fair exchange for our US dollars.

But when I started to board the boat, I got a rude surprise. Looking at all the supplies, then straight into my eyes, the skipper began to sputter. "Hey, lady, this troller…" He took a deep breath and continued. "She is right down to the water line now, it ain't going to hold all that stuff and you too. If you want to take all this, you'll have to find yourself another boat."

With that he stormed down into the boat and pitched out our sleeping bags, tent, camp stove, lanterns and duffel bags, and put them out on the wharf. The more he unloaded the more furious he became. He revved his engine, untied the lines and threw the throttle forward, giving a great wash to the docks.

From the walkway to the store, Roger and Evan yelled, "Why's the boat leaving, Mom?"

Fighting back defeat and disappointment, I shouted back,

"Come on down here and help stack up this stuff and hunt for a new skipper and boat."

An elderly onlooker, who had been standing on the dock watching the drama, then spoke. "Seems you are having a bit of a problem."

"That's an understatement," I replied.

"Maybe I can persuade my son to take you across in his fish boat. Just a minute, and I'll check with him." He walked down to the far end of the dock and disappeared into the wheelhouse of a large fish boat. Immediately the father and son emerged and walked toward us.

"I understand you need to go over to Jedediah Island," said Bud, the younger man.

"Yes," I replied meekly.

"Happens I'm not going out fishing today so I'll take you over."

With this new offer, Roger shouted, "Come on, Evan, let's get this stuff loaded."

"Just a minute, fellows," I said. "How much will the trip cost?"

"Forty dollars will do fine," Bud offered. I agreed, the gear was loaded and we were aboard and on our way.

The trip across Malaspina Strait from Pender Harbour to Texada Island was smooth sailing. Nearing the southern tip of Texada, we rolled with a slight southeasterly. Incoming waves washed the rocky shore.

Evan let out a squeal. "What's that on the rocks?"

"There are often a bunch of sea lions here," the skipper replied. "Some of the males weigh up to two thousand pounds, yet they are very fast in the water. They use their fore flippers for swimming and back ones for rudders. Us fishermen aren't too fond of them as they live well on salmon, herring and other fishes."

He went on to say that we might see some killer whales, too. At this time of year they travelled through this area in groups or pods of five or six or even up to a hundred, and they made quite a sight when they rolled up to the surface and "blew," then sounded deeply underwater. Bud described how often they would leap out of the water, stand on their tails, flap their tail fins and roll, and how a pack of killer whales would sometimes surround a group of smaller whales, as dolphins circle a school of herring and rush in to take their prey. "Once while fishing," he said, "I saw one leap completely out of the water and land on another whale's back. It is known that the killer whale will force open the mouth of another smaller type whale and tear out its tongue, causing the prey to die of shock and loss of blood."

These gory tales of wild whales whipped the boys' interest to a high pitch. Knowing he had their full attention, the skipper continued. "The whales' 30-knot top speed allows them to catch any dolphin, as well as sea lions and marine birds," he said. "They do not seem to relish humans, but attacks on rowboats have been reported, and I have seen the teeth marks." The boys' eyes grew wider.

"Do you see how the shape of Texada is like a huge alligator?" Bud went on. "Point Upwood is the snout and Mount Dick is the head and eye, and farther back is the hump of Mount Shepherd, which rises out of the sea 2,900 feet to the sky."

"Yeah, it sure does look like an alligator," Roger agreed.

"Would one of you boys like to steer the boat while I get up some lines ready for tying up and anchoring?" Bud asked. Both boys rushed to his side. "All right, the youngest should have first turn at the wheel. Now just hold on to the wheel real tight and turn slowly. Just mind that we do not run into any floating logs, or worse, any logs that are half underwater. And keep a straight course for those small islands in front of Jedediah."

Evan never took his eyes from his destination. Sitting tall in the skipper's perch, he was definitely in charge.

After a few minutes the older boy said, "Come on, Evan, you have been steering long enough. My turn now." Usually Evan obeyed his older brother, but this was an exception. Roger persisted, but Evan stood his ground.

I intervened. "Let him steer for a few minutes more."

"Oh, he always gets his way," Roger muttered. Then suddenly he yelled, "You almost hit a log, you nitwit!" He grabbed for the wheel.

"I saw it!" Evan shouted back.

Roger finally had his turn at the wheel and was most pleased to show his skill. His small hands tightened on the wheel as he proudly piloted the fish boat toward the round island at the entrance to Home Bay on Jedediah. The sea was calm, only the lap of the water on the underbelly of the boat could be heard. Chunks of logs and bark floated about, ready to inspect the boat's propeller. The closer we came to the island, the more flotsam and jetsam appeared.

"I guess it's about time to take over now, son," Bud said. Roger reluctantly released the wheel, and he and Evan went out on the deck.

"I have been around the island many times," the skipper told me, "but never sailed into this bay. I am pretty sure there are two or three reefs." He slowed the engine and reached for his marine chart. Pointing to the channel, he explained, "It shows a reef on the east side and two good-sized ones in the centre of the channel." He steadily slowed down the engine and carefully made his way toward shore.

He asked me to go out and watch for any more reefs, and to check the depth of the water. I rushed out of the wheelhouse onto the deck, picked up a pike pole and plunged it down into the water to the bottom of the bay.

The skipper yelled, "How are we doing?"

The rocky outer shore of Jedediah Island.

"We've got about six feet of water yet," I answered. Roger was on the lookout for reefs as well, and with a piece of long rope with a heavy fishing weight on one end he was measuring the depth alongside the boat.

On the island, Jimmy Riddell noticed the fish boat and began rowing out in his small clinker-built rowboat. He pulled up alongside the fish boat and shouted to the skipper, "You're OK, the tide is just turning and coming in, you'll have plenty of water under you in about an hour to come all the way to the float house and unload."

The boys jumped over the side into the water. Thrashing about and squealing how warm the water was, they dove under to bring up sand dollars from the bottom of the bay. Jimmy tied his rowboat alongside and pulled his oars in. Bud reached down to help him board the boat.

"Jim, whatcha doing on Jedediah?" Bud asked.

"So you remember me, Bud, from the days when I fished in

the same waters as you and your dad," Jimmy answered.

"Have you still got the *Quit* with all those pet crows and raccoons aboard?"

"No," Jim replied, "I'm a damn sheep herder now."

"Weren't you living in the Harbour for a while?" Bud inquired.

"Yeah, Mr. and Mrs. Hughes moved to Pender after they sold the island to a Yankee. Jenny at that time needed to be near the St. Mary's hospital on account of her asthma attacks. Mr. Hughes died shortly after they moved to the Harbour and Jenny wished to return to Jedediah, so I moved her with the *Quit*. We built a float house in the bay near her old home. She still makes me live on the *Quit* until Canon Greene drops in to make us man and wife."

Bud threw back his head and laughed. "You lucky old Scotchman," he bellowed, "that she ever considered marrying you at all."

"Enough of your blethering, Bud, come on over to the float house and say hello to Jenny. She always has the kettle on and happy to have visitors, even if it's you."

I agreed to stay aboard the boat while the boys splashed in the water. The two older chaps piled into Jim's rowboat and were off.

As I lounged on the dry deck of the boat watching Roger and Evan, my eyes were drawn to the windswept evergreen firs and pines that clung to the rocky crevices along the shoreline. Looking down through the clear water, I could see flat fishes scurrying around the sandy bottom. The boys made it to shore and began climbing up rock ledges. I shouted, "Don't go far! We all have to help unload the boat."

They yelled back something like "We'll be down by the float house."

The tide was rising swiftly now and Bud and Jimmy were

returning to the fish boat. Bud hopped aboard and started the engine, and the boat floated slowly and steadily along toward Jenny and Jimmy's house. Roger stood on the edge of the float logs and grabbed the tug lines that Bud tossed to him. Everyone pitched in and unloaded the summer supplies.

Jenny noticed our big car battery. "See," she laughed, "you brought along a battery to run your radio on."

"I couldn't forget the battery. The boys have to listen to 'Jack Armstrong, All-American Boy'," I said.

I paid Bud his money in American currency. He looked at the drab green US bills and commented, "Your Yankee money is pretty dull, no colourful pictures on it. Where's the Queen? But I guess I can get rid of it somehow." He laughed, thanked me and gave us all a robust handshake of farewell. We watched as Bud's boat pulled out of the bay into the strait. A few gulls and other seabirds followed as the boat ploughed its way back to Pender Harbour.

"Before you start to take the boxes up to the house, you'd better come in for a cup of tea," Jenny suggested.

The tea was a welcome break before we hauled our supplies up the hill to the old house. When we got there, what a grand surprise awaited us! Jenny and Jimmy had transformed the former dank, dark rooms into bright, livable areas with scrubbing, waxing, painting and wallpapering. A warm, fresh breeze wafted through the open front doorway. A pristine stillness enveloped us.

"Mom, it's so quiet here," whispered my older son. "I can hear my heart beat even."

After a moment, I suggested we choose places to sleep. I didn't want us to put our heads down before the sunlight left us.

"I want the room right in front upstairs," Roger shouted. "I can watch the boats go by and see the mountains on Texada."

Then it was time to find a bit of something to eat before we turned in. Dry paper and kindling had been laid on the grates of the cooking stove, ready to be fired up. I lit the paper and turned away to sort out the groceries. Out went the fire. I found more paper and stuffed it into the firebox, and placed some dry kindling over the paper and a couple of small dry cedar chunks. This time the fire took off and the tea kettle began whistling in the near-dark. Very quickly I was becoming aware that firewood, water and a well-stocked larder were indispensable for island living. At one time, water had been pumped from a natural spring to a large drum fastened to the roof of the house, then it flowed down to the kitchen sink through a pipe. This ancient system had long been rusted out and now water had to be hauled up by hand in buckets. This was a risky chore, as Jimmy kept a frisky black Angus bull in the orchard, which was on the path to the spring. If an apple or other goody was not tossed to the bull, he would charge full bore. After Ed arrived, he installed a ram jet which brought a continuous supply of water from the spring. A small plunger in the ram jet has a compressing effect and forces water to be pumped uphill in a small stream, with no moving parts to break down except a small leather plunger, and no need for fuel.

Gathering wood for the stove and fireplace was a daily chore. Roger scrounged a handmade wheelbarrow from the orchard and filled it with fallen limbs. Evan gathered wood and stacked it into boxes by the stove.

While rowing his boat around the beach, Roger discovered some neat piles of thick, dry bark above the high tide mark on the beach. He threw the bark into the boat and made for the kitchen door. Just then Jimmy was coming up the path and noticed the load of bark. "Say, laddie," he said, "where'd ye find the fine load of bark? Looks like my winter's treasure of bark might be gone, but I know you thought some good elf stacked it on the beach just for the taking." He roared at Roger, "Best pull up your socks and blow your nose and go find your own bark!"

Roger lowered his head. "Sorry, Jimmy," he said. He picked up the handles of the wheelbarrow and left.

"Jim," I said, "how about a cup of tea with me as I sort out what to do next to get things organized."

"Be my pleasure," he replied. "While on the subject of wood, be sure, Mary, that you burn only dry wood, as wet beach wood is filled with salts and will soon put an end to the life of your stove and chimney. Sorry to jump on the lad, but he needs to know the way of island living. Island people are fiercely independent, often stubborn, individualistic and opinionated beyond belief. But it's our way." I filled Jimmy's cup nearly to the top and passed him sugar and a tin of Pacific milk. "I see you found the best tinned milk," Jimmy commented. "You'll find it will keep for months. Also eggs in a solution of silica gel. You will find tinned butter is as fresh as the butter at Lloyd's." Jim placed his empty cup in the sink. "Well, I butchered a deer last night," he continued. "He was into the apple trees in the orchard. He was trespassing and an easy shot. I'll bring you by some this afternoon."

"Oh, that would be great, Jimmy," I said. "Thanks. I haven't had deer meat since I was a kid in the logging camps."

During the first few summer days on the island, the boys and I managed to spread out supplies and stack away our groceries. The radio got hooked up to the car battery and a disk jockey was spinning one of Chubby Checker's platters for the oldest boy. Between the two boys, the stations were switched off and on as fast as a frog on a hot rock. They finally settled for "The Green Hornet," followed by another eerie serial.

At bedtime I suggested they turn off the radio to save the battery, and we'd play rummy before turning in. The kerosene lamp gave just enough of a glow to keep the game going until we all lost interest. Roger headed up the rickety stairs to bed, while

Evan and I made our way out to the two-seater outhouse.

"Hey, Mom, what's that strange sound over there?" It was a soft *say-ee* sound.

I turned the flashlight up through the tree and saw a tiny saw-whet owl. "Oh, Evan, look at the little thing! See his big eyes and small hooked beak. When I was a kid we often had campfires in the evening in the country and these little fellows would perch on a low limb of a tree and keep us company. They are so curious and tame. They clean up mice and other small rodents, and swallow them whole and then spit out the bones and fur."

"What other spooky things are out here at night?"

"Oh, Evan, owls aren't scary. When animals hear us around they are more frightened of us than you should be of them."

We walked back to the house, blew out the lamp and jumped into bed. Thundering tug engines moved through the waters between Jedediah and Texada in a steady rhythm, putting us to sleep.

The next thing I heard was "Big Red," Jimmy's prize rooster, giving his wake-up call. A glimmer of morning sunlight filtered through the thick limbs of a huge fir tree near the bedroom window. I silently made my way to the kitchen. I struck a match to the kerosene lamp and scrounged about for a few sticks of dry kindling. Quickly the kindling crackled and popped and the tea kettle was jumping about in no time. I went out the back door to a bench with a bucket and wash bowl, and splashed my face with cold water. Then I walked down a winding trail to the pastoral plumbing facilities. Our friendly owl was gone. Wild honeysuckle and blackberry vines secluded the outhouse. As I returned to the house, the sound of the creaking step gave way to Roger's voice. "I'm hungry."

"Well, sit down here and have a bowl of cooked oatmeal with brown sugar and canned milk," I said.

"Gosh, Mom, you know I don't like mush."

"Sorry, son, but that's it." After mounds of brown sugar were stacked on, the oatmeal vanished.

After the boys had eaten, I announced that we needed to get a routine of chores going in the morning. "Roger, you bring up four buckets of water from the spring and Evan, you cut and stack kindling in the woodbox until it's full. Then we'll all go hunting for dry wood and stack it in the woodshed."

Packing buckets of water up from the spring was a heavy-duty chore. The boys didn't quarrel over who would cut kindling—each one had a bright shiny new hatchet and hunting knife which needed a piece of wood to work on.

"Remember, boys, if you cut yourself or break a leg, I'll have to shoot you, as there's no way to get help." This wasn't an altogether idle threat. While Jimmy's fish boat the *Quit* was anchored in the bay, half the time the tide was out and it was high and dry. It could take hours to reach the hospital at Pender Harbour. One mile away, at Rouse Bay on Lasqueti Island, a cable phone line to the mainland had been laid on the bottom of the ocean floor. This phone was located out on a rock at the entrance to the bay. It was used mainly in emergencies by storm-bound and battered sea-going souls, by fishermen and tourists in times of distress. This was the time in island life before CBs or VHF radio communications were available.

Old log barn on Jedediah, built in 1908.

After breakfast and the chores were finished, the boys ran down to the beach and jumped into an old rowboat that Jimmy had rescued from a winter's storm. Apparently it had freed itself from a larger boat. I yelled at them, "Get back here and put on your life jackets." They knew the rules of never going out in a boat without a life jacket and an extra oar.

Each had a sturdy jigging line and a heavy hook. Jimmy rigged the gear for the boys so they could catch bottom fish such as rock cod. Once a week if the sea was calm, Jimmy took Roger along with him to Lasqueti to collect the mail, and they fished coming and going. One rowed the boat and the other held the fish line, and if only one of them was in the boat, he wrapped the line around his leg and pulled it along behind the boat while he rowed. When he felt a strike, he jerked the line, quit rowing and hopefully pulled in the fish.

While the boys were fishing, I busied myself in attempting to make bread. In my collection of gear I had brought along instruction books on how to make bread, churn butter, spin and weave wool, along with medical procedures on delivering babies (which I had occasion to use), setting bones, applying a tourniquet and remodelling old houses, barns, etc.

Finally I settled on a simple recipe for making whole wheat bread. Reading it over, I judged that I could make a few improvements by adding an extra pinch of this and that. While I was mixing, pounding and kneading, Jenny appeared at the kitchen door. "I hope I'm not intruding," she said shyly.

"Oh no, Jenny. It's a joy to have you, especially when I'm trying to make my first batch of bread."

"Is that whole wheat bread you're making?" She came closer to the gummy mess. "Would you mind if I got my hands into it?"

"Not at all."

She washed up and began to throw the dough, beads of perspiration forming on her forehead as she pounded the dough,

Jenny Hughes cutting into an enormous log on Jedediah, 1930s.

added more flour and water, then shaped it into a large, round mass. This she covered with a damp cloth and placed high on a shelf over the cooking stove, to rise.

"Oh, Jenny, I haven't made bread since I left my mother's kitchen," I said.

"Guess not," was her response.

We sat down for a cup of tea and Jenny started to roll a homemade cigarette.

"That's a strange-looking tobacco," I commented.

"Mary, it isn't tobacco," she answered, "it's chicory. I grow it in my garden and dry it in the summer in the barn." She inhaled a few puffs and said, "Is there anything Jimmy and I could help you with?"

"You and Jimmy have been so wonderful to clean and polish the old house," I said. "We are very cozy and comfortable. I won't have a thing to do now."

Jenny threw back her head and laughed. "Don't worry

about things to do," she said. "You'll never find enough time to do what is even necessary." Looking around the open kitchen, her huge sea-blue eyes twinkled. "I've spent the happiest years of my life in this room, enjoying new and old friends. Fellow workers from the hospital in Vancouver came to see Mr. Hughes and me soon after we were married. Many still sail here for grand times. Summertimes were filled with yachtsmen, in spring and fall, fishermen and tugboat men dropped in while waiting for storms to abate. Winters were less long with local folks venturing over. You always knew your best friends would brave the heavy winds and rains to make the trip." Slowly Jenny arose from her chair, tossed her cigarette butt into the firebox of the stove and said, "I'd best be getting down to the garden. Is there something like lettuce or carrots you would like?"

"No thanks, but I really would like to walk with you and perhaps help you weed or whatever needs to be done," I suggested.

Our backs were warmed by the midmorning sun as we strolled along through the orchard. The fruit trees had just lost their blossom and tiny apples, pears and plums were forming.

"There were a lot of cherries this spring, but these devils the crows got most of them," Jenny scoffed. She kept a swift pace and as she got closer to the garden I had difficulty keeping up with her. As we climbed over the steps that straddle the fence, our shoes sunk into wet spongy black soil. Rows of cabbages, carrots, beets, lettuce, chard and peas, along with many interesting herbs, were thriving.

"How do you get cabbages like this?" I asked as I weeded around a plant at least two feet across.

"Loads and loads of chicken, sheep, cow and horse manure feeds a fine garden, plus loads of back-breaking labour, along with a bit of luck and knowledge. To live here year round, you must be as self-sufficient as possible—and growing a garden is very necessary."

As we weeded up and down rows of vegetables, Jenny asked whether we were intending to make Jedediah our permanent home.

"We hope to someday," I answered, "but for now we are going to spend a summer or two and get acquainted with this way of life. Also to find out how our boys adapt to isolation, and how correspondence school suits them. Jenny, do you know of any children in this area who learn well with the correspondence type of school?"

"Yes, if you contact the Department of Education in Victoria, they will give you all the information. You understand I didn't have children, but the people who lived on Jedediah before Mr. Hughes had small children and I believe they had correspondence schooling." She continued as she weeded. "You know there are a great deal of things to consider with such a big move. However, I think you are going about it wisely by taking your time in changing your way of life."

Suddenly Evan came running down the path to the garden, hollering all the way and holding up a scrawny, prickly, bug-eyed fish. He was overjoyed. Jenny and I joined in the chorus, exclaiming, "Boy, that's a dandy of a fish!"

"Cook it for lunch, Mom!"

"OK."

We headed toward the house. Roger came up from the dock, trudged into the kitchen and asked, "What's for lunch?"

"Fish," I replied.

"Not that horrible thing Evan brought up from the bottom?"

"It's better than you got!" Evan shouted back at him. "Nothing!"

"Well, the real fish weren't biting, or I would have landed us a good feed."

After lunch we took a hike. I took along a pail just in case we ran into a berry patch. The boys ran on ahead. I cautioned them to be quiet running through the brush as we might see some goats or deer if we were careful. We hiked over a moss-covered hill and crept down into a deep valley which was lush with high-growing ferns, salal, reeds and other heavy undergrowth. I pressed my finger to my lips and whispered, "See the goats ahead on that knoll?" Eighteen or twenty sleek black and brown goats with great twisted horns were grazing on the underbrush, unaware of our presence. My feet dislodged a loose rock and as it went tumbling down, a big billy gave a warning snort and they all dashed down the hill.

"Whee, what's the stink?" Evan squealed.

"It's the goats. Usually you smell them before you see them."

On the way down from the top of the hill we found a generous patch of blackberries ripe and ready for picking. Each of us ate two berries to every one we put into the pail, yet we filled it up quickly. As twilight enfolded us, I said, "Come on, fellas, we'd better get back to the house."

When we reached the kitchen, every corner was dark. I fumbled about and found the kerosene lamp and matches. The soft light from the lamp reflected eerie images on the tongue-and-groove panelled wall. To cheer up the scene, I started a fire in the cook stove and filled the black iron frying pan with popping corn.

"Let's play a game of cards," I suggested.

Evan got the cards out and dealt each of us a rummy hand. Before my turn I jumped up and shook the frying pan ferociously as the corn popped.

"Hey, Evan, that's not the right suit," Roger complained. "You've got two spades and one club. Yeah, I know they are both black, but that don't count."

"Here, have some popcorn," I offered. "I'll help Evan count his cards. Soon he'll be able to play better." The card game went on until we had trouble seeing the cards.

"I'm going to bed," Roger announced.

"I'm not tired," Evan mumbled.

"Guess it's time to blow out the lantern and off with all of us."

Chapter

2

THE MORNING WAS BRIGHT, SUNNY AND WARM. All was stillness, not a ripple on the water.

"Boys, how would you like to go exploring?" I said. "I'll pack a lunch and we'll investigate some of the other islands around us." We three jumped into the rowboat and Roger put his weight against the oars.

"Put on your life jackets," I ordered.

In the bottom of the boat was a fishing pole with a line attached that was tangled beyond belief. I pulled the line back and forth, in and out until it was straightened out. I secured the sinker and flasher and retied the hook, then let the line sink down beside the boat. Down, down it went until I could feel the action of the flasher. Now for the big awaited strike. Evan began to squeal. "The seal over there!" He pointed to the sleek head of a seal. Its large pop eyes watched us carefully, then quietly it sank backwards into the water. Soon it bobbed up again in curiosity, exposing its round, smooth head. Its eyes and nostrils were situated high on its head, enabling the animal to see and breathe while exposing a minimum of its body, and to be ever ready for a deep dive. I pulled in my fishing line as Mr. Seal would be the first to pull in my fish, if I got lucky.

"Let's row over to that small reef that looks like it's white-washed," I suggested.

"Look at all the birds on it!"

As we approached the small island, several black birds with a greenish sheen on their feathers took off and then dived into the water.

Roger (standing on pier) and Evan, 1950. The boys' "putt-putt boat" was their main method of transportation around the coast of Jedediah and nearby islands.

"Those are cormorants," I told the boys. "They are diving for fish. They can stay under water for almost a minute, then after several dives they perch out of the water and fluff their wings, which helps restore the trapped air which has been expelled from their feathers by water pressure. See, there is one going under again." Along with the cormorants were many gulls, scoters, oystercatchers and murrelets riding high on the water.

"Watch the murrelets dive. They give a quick forward flip, and their fat behinds bob up."

Close to our boat a group of small gulls bounced on the surface, probably Bonaparte gulls. They had black heads and their wings and upper bodies were bluish-grey. "When you see these gulls," I told the boys, "you know a school of fish has been forced to the surface by feeding salmon. The gulls feed on the herring along with other small fishes which come to the top of the water to avoid the salmon."

"Boy, if we see these gulls we better get fishing," Evan said.

I offered to row for a while but Roger said he was all right. "Anyway I'd like to row into Bull Island for a look and a visit," he said. "Jimmy and I pass here when we go for the mail and Jimmy says there are a bunch of kids living there. Let's go in and visit them."

I wasn't too keen on seeing anyone, I just wanted to investigate the islands. But I nodded and Roger slowed down on the oars and we drifted onto a small gravelly beach. Spilling out the doorway of a beached float house, browned, bare siblings bounced along a board plank that reached from the door of their float house to the beach. Some swam out to meet our boat while others shyly hung behind the driftwood that decorated the beach.

A smiling lady waved and greeted us. "Come on in," she called.

Evan and Roger leaped out of the boat and began swimming around with the young ones. I threw out a small anchor to keep the boat from leaving with the outgoing tide, and I tumbled out of the boat. We were all surrounded by warm, giggling girls, and a boy about age ten was showing us his skills as a swimmer and diver. He would wade out into the bay with a large rock held against his chest until he came to a drop off, then go down with the rock and stay under until everyone yelled and struggled to pull him out of the water—great sport for him!

"Top of the morning to you," the woman smiled. "My name is Helen Ryan. I'm the mother of this motley crew." She laughed as she wiped her hands on her apron, which was fastened tightly to her well-worn dress with safety diaper pins. Helen was petite and pleasingly plump, and her curly light brown hair was tossed about her head. I followed her up the plank to a landing where a water hose was fastened to a board with a sink under it. On one side was a gasoline-powered washing machine thrashing about with great agitation.

Helen Ryan. Art and Helen Ryan and their ten children were good friends who lived on Bull Island.

"My husband Art is up in the bush logging the other side of the island. Come on into the kitchen and I'll put the kettle on." The kitchen was long and narrow. In the centre of the room stood a large table with benches and boxes piled beneath. Against the back wall a huge cast-iron stove was covered with copper boilers. Pots and pans were filled with steaming wash water. Under the stove, cats of different descriptions were sleeping. "Are you the new people from Jedediah?"

"That's us," I answered, sitting down on a box next to the table. "We hope to spend a summer or two here, then settle permanently. One of my main concerns is schooling for my boys. How do you handle schooling for your bunch?"

"I try to teach mine by correspondence, but with so many little ones, eight girls and two boys, I really don't find time and energy to do a proper job of it."

"I can see you have your hands full, all right."

Helen poured steaming hot water into a brown betty teapot. "If you move here with your two boys we could set up a school here," she said. "There is a small shed up the hill back of the float house that my husband could repair and make into a schoolhouse, if you would be willing to take on the task of teaching the beggars." Helen took papers and leaves from a large tin of tobacco and rolled a cigarette.

"Sounds great to me, but it will take a bit of planning and will depend on if we move to Jedediah year round," I replied.

Pounding bare feet could be heard on the plank walk leading to the house, and the tiny room was quickly filled with dripping wet young bodies. Inquisitive glances were cast upon me, and a muscular little girl jumped up onto my lap, looked deeply into my eyes, pulled my face toward hers and asked, "What's your name?"

"Mary," I answered.

"My name's Valerie," she laughed.

"Settle down, Valerie. Get off her lap and put on some dry clothes," Helen demanded. The older girls were leaning on or sitting around the table, ready for tea and conversation. Under our feet on the bare floor, arms and legs flew in all directions and howls and screams filled the room.

"Hey, Sidney, leave Arthur alone," was heard above the din. Poor Arthur was the youngest of the two boys, and the girls played with him like a doll, dressing him up in their clothes and giving him little peace. Apparently he spent most of his time hiding from them under the kitchen stove. Sidney, the older boy and the great underwater swimmer, went crashing over to a shelf by the one big window in the kitchen and reached up to find a box filled with his treasures. Opening the box, he yelled, "Who the devil has been in my stuff? They took my best hooks." He swung around and grabbed one of the girls by her long hair, then pulled her into a corner and began to trounce her. Mayhem broke loose. Helen jumped up and pulled Sidney off Barbara. She threw him out the door and down the plank, and then she screeched, "Now the rest of you little beasts clear out. We would like some time to ourselves." Helen apologized to me, explaining that the children didn't see many people and got pretty wound up when someone dropped by. The oldest girl tarried just outside the doorway, her azure blue eyes cast downward, her slight body clothed loosely with a faded, rust-coloured dress. A piece of worn pink ribbon tied back her long blonde hair.

One of the other girls called to her. "Beverly, come on, Roger wants to take us rowing in his boat." She skipped away to join her sister.

"Why do the girls seem to pair off in twos?" I asked Helen.

Helen refilled my granite tea cup as she rolled another cigarette. "They do pair off for close companionship. If a third joins in often it leads to quarrels, yet there are times when the whole crew sings along together."

"How do you get all your supplies to the island, Helen?"

"With such a large vegetable garden, we really need very little in town. I put up hundreds of bottles of vegetables. We have a few fruit trees and berries, and Art fishes when he isn't logging, and he hunts for our fair share of deer. When we need staples such as tea, coffee, sugar and flour, we go in the *Montana*, Art's fish boat, to Nanaimo and pick them up."

I stood up. "I'd better check on my boys and see how far they are rowing the girls." I yelled out the open window, "Don't go out of the bay in that boat."

"OK," was the faint reply.

As I pulled in my head, my eyes fell on a piece of cream-coloured paper thumbtacked to the wall. It was a cheque for $7,400, dated several months before.

"Helen!" I gasped. "Sorry I noticed, but how can you leave

Rub-a-dub-dub, three Ryans in a tub, 1956. Sharon, Karen and Sidney enjoy a fresh-air bath.

a big cheque like this pinned to the wall? It sure isn't any of my business, but you should put it in a safe place."

"Well, you see, I don't have any other safe place to hide it that the kids won't get into it. If it's on the wall I can see it all the time. Art hasn't had a chance to go to town to put it in the bank but he'll be going in a few days. Mary, can you and the boys stay for dinner? We are going to barbecue a deer on the beach."

"We sure would love to stay," I said, "if you let me help you."

Heavy caulk boots were heard pounding on the plank leading to the kitchen door, and Art appeared on the landing. Tall, thin and muscular, he unlaced his boots and kicked them off. Then he bent over the sink and began to splash water all over his upper body. Wiping dry with a towel, he came into the kitchen, put out his hand and greeted me with, "I'm only the dad and skipper of this crew. Art Ryan," he said. "I've got a lot of trees down and ready to drag into the channel," he told Helen. "I'll need a boom man in a day or two. Is the mowitch ready for the fire?"

"Yeah," Helen answered. "The kids and I have him down on the beach ready for the spit."

We all made our way down to the beach as Sid made a roaring fire in the pit. Art placed a heavy wire grid over the pit and spread large portions of the venison on the grid. Juices began to ooze from the meat.

"How do you like yours?" Art asked. "Dripping in blood?"

"Oh, no," I shuddered. "But not charcoal, either."

Several of the little ones watched the barbecue as a light breeze wafted the delicious odour about. "Golly, Mom, we're hungry."

"OK then, run up to the garden and bring down the spuds I dug this morning, and pick some ripe corncobs too."

Off they flew. Helen cut slices of whole wheat bread. Berry jam and other goodies were arranged on pieces of flat driftwood. Blue granite plates, cups and cutlery were spread before us. Whole potatoes were tossed on the coals along with unshelled corn.

"You're gonna burn your spud if you don't get it out of the fire!"

"Oh, mind your own stuff."

Art pulled a hind leg off the grid and everyone gathered around as he carved it with his sharp hunting knife into portions great enough to satisfy Henry the Eighth. My potato was black and burned on the outside and hard as a rock inside, just as I had expected. The corn was heavenly. Linda, one of the older girls, pointed to Roger and laughed. "Look how he eats his corn. He goes around and around instead of sideways along the whole cob. Guess it's the Yankee way of eating corn." All the little ones shouted with laughter.

It was the first time I had had venison since I was a kid, during the Depression years of the 1930s, living out in the wilderness of the Olympic Mountains. It was about all the meat we had, as I recalled.

"We usually have either mowitch or fish to eat," Helen said. "Sometimes clams or oysters fill in, but some of the kids aren't too keen on shellfish, especially Karen, the littlest."

Boiling hot tea and peanut butter cookies finished the outdoor meal. "Time for us to head back to Jedediah boys," I urged as the rosy sky darkened.

"Oh, can't we stay a little longer, Mom?" they both pleaded. "Stay longer!" echoed among all the Ryans. We crouched down around the glowing embers of the fire, in a state of euphoria. Theresa, Colleen, Linda and Sid skipped flat rocks on the surface of the still water. Irene, Barbara, Beverley and Valerie stacked the plates, cups, forks and knives into neat piles and took them up to the float house.

Our small rowboat floated along the surface of the water with the tide as it came to the edge of the beach, ready for boarding. Art held the boat steady and we stepped in. "Are you and the boys alone on the island?" he asked.

"No, Art, we have Jenny and Jimmy. They're living in their float house. In a few days my husband Ed will be with us too. He is still in Seattle getting our boat engine in good running order. It gave out on our way here, and he had to stay to get it repaired. I look for him to sail into Home Bay anytime now." I adjusted the oars in the oarlocks. "We sure miss him, but we know he will be along just as soon as he can."

"If you need any help over on the island, be sure to call on us here," Art offered.

"Thanks, Art, I appreciate it." Three or four of the Ryan children waded out alongside the boat as we made ready for departure. I yelled back, "Thanks, Helen and Art, for a most wonderful time. We'll not forget this day. Come over to Jedediah as soon as you can."

I strained on the oars to help work off the huge amount of food I had enjoyed. As we approached Jedediah, Evan pointed to the shore and shouted, "See the goats!" Glistening coats of chestnut brown and black covered their large bodies. A few strands of hair hung down from their underbellies and chins, and their horns pointed backwards over their rumps. They continued to forage until one huge male put his nose in the air and gave a grunting sort of whistle, and off they all charged through the bush and out of sight.

"You know, boys," I commented, "Jimmy told me the Spanish explorers brought the first goats to the island. They

The Spanish explorers who visited the BC coast in the eighteenth century kept goats aboard ship for meat and milk. Some historians believe that the goats were put off to graze when the crew made short side trips, and that some of the goats never made it back on board. Their descendants still live on Jedediah.

kept goats aboard their ships for milk and meat and put them off to graze while they ventured farther along the coast. On their journey south, they picked up a few for the crew's needs."

The boys and I found the days melted into each other too swiftly. We were up in the morning when the sun glistened over Mount Dick on Texada Island. We'd go down to the spring for buckets of water, a quick wash or sponge bath by the kitchen door, and then splinter a few pieces of dry cedar for starting the fire in the cooking stove. Soon the coffee pot was steaming and the pail of bubbling hot water was ready for the Red River cereal.

One day all was perking and steaming when I heard the roar of an airplane motor overhead. Roger yelled from upstairs, "Oh hey, Mom, is that a plane?"

"Yes, and it's circling over us," I replied.

Evan was up and running outdoors to check the plane, which hovered and landed just outside the bay as I reached the shore. Roger ran down to the float, jumped into the rowboat and rowed out to meet it. As we all had hoped, it was Dad. Ed piled from the plane to the boat with all his gear. Evan and I could hear them shouting and laughing from the shore. The float plane took off with a thundering roar.

Ed had brought us many store-bought goodies. "Oh look, Mom, a big brick of ice cream!" Evan squealed. I quickly unwrapped the ice cream, which was covered with layers of newspaper. The brick was already a bit soft, so I spooned it into dishes.

"Please Evan, run these two dishes of ice cream down to the float house to Jenny and Jimmy," I said.

"Oh, Mom, Roger will eat all the ice cream while I'm gone."

"Oh no he won't. Now get going."

He was back in a flash.

"I believe the boys miss their ice cream, hamburgers and french fries most," I told Ed. "However, I have a treat. Art Ryan from Bull Island brought us over some fine venison. I have ground it up with the meat grinder, made some hamburger buns and dug a few of Jenny's potatoes, so now we can also enjoy drive-in fare."

As we sat around the kitchen table enjoying our special lunch, Ed explained that he had become disenchanted with the *PBY* and sold it quickly to an admirer. He contended that it was best we all fly in and out for the summers, or hire a water taxi, until we could get a seaworthy craft under us. "I left the nursery and landscape crew in care of George," he said, "and hope to stay here on the island with you all for at least a couple of weeks. You and the boys can stay until school begins in September, if you like."

Roger, Evan and I enjoy one of many peaceful summer moments on Jedediah, 1950.

"We like!" was heard in two-part harmony. Ed jumped up from the kitchen table, threw Evan up in the air over his head, and said, "Hey, fella, let's get the chores done and go for a hike up to the top of the island." We all rallied around and washed the dishes with water heated on top of the stove, rinsed them and let them dry. Leftover food was stored in the screened cooler on the back porch. The fire in the cooking stove was extinguished, as it is foolish and sometimes fatal to leave a burning fire in an unattended house.

We scrambled through blackberry brambles and thick

passages of salal and fern, pushing forward and upward, sometimes on our hands and knees. To reach the highest point on the island takes a bit of doing for two boys aged five and nine and a couple in their thirties. Looking back over my shoulder, I saw Evan completely lost in a hole covered with ferns. "Help, help, I'm stuck!" he was screeching. Ed thrashed his way over and pulled him out, threw him on his shoulders and pushed on through the underbrush. Our hiking boots sunk deeply into the soft spongy moss that covered the many mounds and hills along the way.

I suggested a minute's rest. Roger unstrapped his trusty World War II canteen filled with water, took a long drink and passed it to his brother. He was very proud of this canteen, which he had found while poking around at an army surplus outlet with his dad. He strapped it to his thick leather belt whenever he was adventuring. We all lay back in the moss, drenched in the warm sunlight. The breeze brought us the distinct odour of goats, and sure enough eight or nine of them were grazing nearby. The leader, a huge billy, started down the hill and the rest followed slowly. Once or twice they turned around and twisted their long horns to take another look at us. We climbed on and gradually the underbrush gave way to dwarfed, gnarly pines and stunted arbutus trees. Sunken pools choked with ferns and reeds provided water for the feral goats, deer and other creatures.

Roger was the first to reach the summit of Gibraltar. He placed another flat stone on top of the cairn that former climbers had built to mark the summit. Through the years, hikers had added their names and dates to a long list in a sealed glass jar at the base of the cairn. Looking to the west, we could see down into the bay of Bull Island and make out figures on the beach. The smoke from Helen's kitchen stove swirled upwards to the sky. Turning to look to the northwest, we admired Trematon Mountain on Lasqueti Island.

Gibraltar, the highest point on Jedediah. When Ed and I first climbed it (the highest point is 500 feet above sea level), we found a cairn and a small notebook and pencil recording the names of those who had reached the top before us, starting with the Footes, Jellys and Olmsteads before World War I.

Directly southeast, Mount Baker shone like a magnificent ice cream cone in the sunlight. As we started down, sometimes sliding on the seats of our pants, we looked skyward to see a seaplane circling the island. The boys urged us on with "Hurry up, let's see who it is." In the undergrowth we found an old logging skid road that was nearly buried in the swampy ground. Jenny had told us that in the early 1900s, Japanese loggers selectively logged part of the island. Oxen pulled the cut logs to the water over skid roads made of cedar slabs that were greased heavily. The logs were boomed in a bay on the west side of Jedediah and towed to a mill. The Japanese had contracted for the timber from the homesteader, Harry John Foote. Some of the timber had been used to build the house at Home Bay.

As we approached the pasture, Jimmy ran toward us, gasping. "I think we have a dead man on the float, or he is dead drunk." He stopped to take a deep breath. "The pilot of the float plane was told to take him here."

We all rushed down to the float and found Jenny bending over the body of a huge man. She was struggling to loosen his collar. His bulky frame thrashed about in his suit as his gnarled hand reached for his head and he muttered, "Back to camp... Gotta get the boys back on the job."

"God, he must be from across the way on Texada, at the logging outfit," said Jimmy. "Best roll him over into the skiff and take him over there to check." Ed, Jimmy and Roger tugged, pulled and pushed him into the boat. All the while he was moaning, "Gotta get the boys going."

On the rocky beach on Texada, two burly fellows removed the boss from the bottom of the boat. He came to long enough to grunt a thanks. One of the loggers muttered that the pilot must have been a new one, as the regular one knew where he

A view into Home Bay, 1907. The wood-frame house was built that year by Harry John Foote, born in London in 1859. Many decades later, it became our home.

came from. After a few days' break in town, seeing the bright lights and enjoying the high life, quite a few of the fellows needed a pilot who knew which camp they belonged to.

"Where did you find Irving?" one of the workers asked.

"Right on my float," Jimmy answered, "across the way on Jedediah."

"Well, we sure are glad you figured out where he belonged. He's the one who runs the show here and keeps the operation going full bore."

"He's all yours now," Jimmy said.

Rowing back through the Sabine Channel, Jimmy filled the air with expletives that would shame his fellow Scotsmen.

"Damn drunken loggers raping the whole coast of its virgin timber, then leaving a mess. Sure, fishermen take their share of booty too but under controlled regulations." Roger took over the rowing and let Jimmy cool down.

That evening, as we enjoyed dinner at the old house with Jenny and Jimmy, Jenny asked, "Will you be leaving Jedediah soon?"

Ed dug into his second piece of blackberry pie before answering, "I'll have to go in a few days," he said, "but Mary and the boys can stay on until the end of August."

"When you gonna get back?" Jimmy inquired.

Ed hesitated, then answered, "I'm not sure."

"Well, Ed, I'll be going over to Lasqueti for mail in a day or two. From there you can get a ride up to False Bay on the north end of the island. A fellow named Domville has a water taxi which will take you to French Creek close to Parksville, and from there you can catch a bus to Vancouver or Victoria."

"Sounds like a real adventure," Ed answered. "I'll take you up on the offer."

Shadows filtered through the kitchen as dusk closed in. Jenny finished her tea, stood up tall and reached for her wool sweater, and Jimmy snuffed out his cigarette and slowly creaked out of his chair. "I'll let you know when I go for the mail," he said. "It'll probably be in a day or two."

We awoke with the humming of an outboard motor in the bay. It was Art Ryan, from Bull Island. We all ran down to the beach to greet him. As he threw out his anchor chain I introduced Ed to Art, and Art invited Ed to Bull Island to see the hand-logging show there. The boys pleaded to go along, but I reminded them that sometimes adults like to be on their own.

"Let's go fishing," I suggested to them. "You boys get the fishing gear ready and go down to the boat and bail it out, while I clean up the kitchen." I made a few sandwiches and packed a few bottles of homemade root beer into a sack, and off we went. The water was calm, the sky cloudless and blue. Looking out over the water, I saw a movement. Then Evan squealed, "Look! What's that?"

"It looks like a porpoise," I replied. The creature leaped out of the water, showing a black head with a white underside. It was longer than our rowboat. We were silent in wonderment, half frightened it would return and half hoping it would. It didn't.

Fishing was poor. We all tried jigging for rock fish and came up with three or four. Rock fish live on the bottom and require fishing down among the reefs below, which claim a fair share of fishing tackle. Hook, line and sinker can easily become entangled among underwater rocky crevices and seaweed, and be lost forever.

Art returned Ed that evening, just at dusk. The boys and I were playing cards when he bolted through the kitchen door, a big grin on his face covering up his torn shirt, ripped pants and worn boots.

Ed threw back his head and laughed. "Boy what a day! Those guys really know how to work! Sidney is a great help to his dad too, along with Louie, a cousin of Helen's. Two men and

Sidney, Barbara and Colleen Ryan with "BS Louie," Helen's cousin, 1950.

a boy can pull out a lot of timber in a day." Ed explained that Art had an easy show in Little Bull Pass, dropping the logs and booming for towing to the mill in Nanaimo. He burned the bucked up limbs and slash when he was through. In time new seedlings would appear and grow, but it took fifty to seventy years for top timber to be ready for cutting again.

As Ed washed up, he asked, "Did Jimmy say when he would be going to Lasqueti?"

"Yes, he said he would go about noon tomorrow, as the tide is in enough to float the rowboat so he can row out of the bay easily."

"I'd best go over with him then. I'm a bit worried about how the business is faring these days with us away."

"Oh, they'll get along without us for a while," I murmured. The boys put the cards away and we had a quick snack of oatmeal cookies and hot chocolate before bedding down for the night.

After breakfast Jimmy was at the back door. "Ready for mail day? I'll take the *Quit* so we all can go over for a visit with the Phillips family at Rouse Bay." The tide brought the water in the bay high enough so Jimmy could get the *Quit* off its "cradle," a wooden support that kept the boat upright when the tide receded.

We were all aboard when the one-lunger gasoline Vivian engine throbbed and vibrated, thrusting us forward out of the bay on our way to Lasqueti. Jimmy eased the *Quit* by Rabbit, Sheer, Circle (called "Round" by locals) and Bull islands along the route to Lasqueti. The sea was still. Gulls followed us and big billowy clouds

Roger with friends at Rouse Bay on Lasqueti Island, 1951.

above danced lightly through an azure sky. Before us a concrete marker pointed to the entrance to Rouse Bay. The bay was named for Bill Rouse, an early settler on Lasqueti Island who raised sheep and other livestock during the 1800s. He rowed or sailed a small boat from Lasqueti to Nanaimo to sell his goods.

On the beach we found Edward Phillips working on his new wooden boat, the *VIP*. As soon as he saw the *Quit* he dropped his tools and ran down to the edge of the water to help Jimmy anchor out. Everyone disembarked from the *Quit* to the row-boat and we made our way to the beach. Up from the beach a few yards was a lovely rustic home. At an open doorway stood a tiny, pleasant, middle-aged woman with black kinky hair that was pinned back in a chignon. Her skin glistened a dark olive, pulled tightly over her high cheekbones. Extending her small hand to mine she said, "I'm Evadne Phillips, and this is my niece Diane, and my mother."

A tea tray filled with yummy pastries was whisked before us. Evadne poured steaming hot tea from a blue porcelain teapot into matching cups and saucers. We were surrounded by warm, friendly people of culture in a world of wilderness.

Evadne asked, "How are you folks doing on Jedediah?"

"It's heavenly," I answered. "We are really enjoying our stay."

"I really hate to leave, but I must be getting back to Seattle," Ed chimed in. "Mary and the boys will remain for the rest of the summer."

"You probably know we have been here for only a short time too," said Evadne. "We came originally from British Guiana and located for a short time in New York, before coming to Lasqueti. Our home is happily shared with Mr. Sweet. George came to us when he reached his golden years."

A tall, thin man entered the room and introduced himself as George Sweet. George knew Jedediah well as he had pre-empted Bull Island, next to Jedediah, in 1910, just after he finished his service in the Boer War. It was difficult to imagine this pale, thin man as a warrior. He took out a package of cigarette papers and began to roll his own. In a low voice he offered Jimmy a cigarette, then rolled another and held it out to Ed, who declined graciously.

Jimmy vigorously slapped George on the knee. "George and I have fished together for many years up and down the coast as well as being neighbours," he remarked laughingly. "My wife and I pre-empted Jenkins Island beside Lasqueti in the spring of 1907. Remember the time, George, when we had a slow fishing day? I took all my caught fish from the hold, strung them on a

Evadne and Edward Phillips (at right), our neighbours on Lasqueti Island, with friends, 1940s. The silver-haired man in the middle is George Sweet, who pre-empted Bull Island in 1910.

line and lowered them into the chuck, just as your boat the *Bridgewater* was coming alongside. I pulled the line up and lo and behold, only fish heads remained. A fat smiling seal had the last laugh on me."

The boys were fascinated by the fish stories and Evadne's goodies, but soon their attention was drawn to the beach where two little girls were playing in the sand and they went off to join them.

"Would you all like to see my garden?" Evadne asked.

We all walked up a slight hill to a well-kept garden. "Your apple trees are really filled, Evadne," Jimmy remarked.

"Yes, it seems to be a great year for the fruit trees. Wait till you see the corn—it's sky high already. Everyone helped me gather starfish from the sea, and I dug them down deep in the planting holes before I seeded this spring."

Her garden was very special—not a weed in sight, and cultivated to the highest degree. Rows and rows of thriving vegetables and herbs were there to be admired. Along the neat edges of the garden, flowers showed their colours. Evadne pulled up a few carrots, beets and a couple heads of lettuce for us to take back to Jedediah. "I know Jenny has many fine vegetables to share with you," she said, "but I enjoy sharing a bit too."

Jimmy asked if Edward would mind taking Ed up to False Bay to catch Domville's water taxi so he could reach Vancouver Island.

"I'll be glad to," Edward answered. "Just have to get the old truck fired up and we can leave." Ed returned to the house to say farewell and the rest of us tagged along, including the boys and two little girls from the beach. Ed gave the boys and me a big hug and into the truck he jumped. We all watched as the truck chugged up the dirt road and rambled out of sight. Jenny and Jimmy picked up their mail from Evadne's kitchen table. We all leisurely strolled about the lawn and flower gardens in the front of the house.

Jenny bent down to admire the lilies in bloom. "Evadne," she said, "remember the slips you gave me from your lilac? They all took root and are growing into lovely flowering shrubs now."

All too soon it was time to call the boys to get ready to board the *Quit*. Everyone walked down the path to the beach and helped us board the dinghy, where Jimmy was already in the wheelhouse starting the Vivian.

We all settled on the deck of the old fishing boat to watch

the glorious sunset over the water. When we arrived in Home Bay the tide was out, so the boys and I jumped over the side of the *Quit* into the shallow water of the tide flats. Jenny and Jimmy stayed aboard to follow the tide in slowly so the boat could rest on its cradle at high tide. A carpet of sand dollars covered the floor of the bay. The live ones were flat, circular and velvety appearing. The dead ones were empty white shells. Evan ran over and picked up a handful to add to his overflowing beach collection. Roger pulled a mammoth starfish from its footing and explained, "Did you know if you cut off one of their arms it will grow another to replace it, and when they try to eat a clam that is too big, they can digest the clam outside their body, and after the clam is eaten the stomach returns to its normal place?"

"Oh, Roger, you sure can tell a story," Evan laughed.

"No, its true, I read it in a science book."

As we made our way through the low water, we couldn't help but step on oysters, as they were everywhere. We climbed the path to the house. Dry cedar kindling gave us a quick fire and soon dinner was ready. The scene was somehow silent and lonely without Ed.

Early the next morning Jimmy awoke us to say he was taking Jenny to Pender Harbour. She had suffered greatly in the night with an asthma attack.

"Jimmy, could I be of any help?" I asked.

"No, thanks," he replied. "I plan to take her over in the *Quit*. I'll let you know about her as soon as we can."

Without the *Quit* they would have to rely on a makeshift method of emergency help, by putting a white sheet on top of the roof of the house, or hanging a large white cloth on the end of a pole like a flag. Tugboat men or fishermen with radiophones would call for help for the distressed family if they saw a white banner, a method of emergency communication used frequently

Jimmy Riddell (second from left), Roger (middle) and Evan (right) with the caretakers of Jedediah and a relative, 1950s.

along the coast before CBs or VHF systems came into use.

We all waved to Jenny and Jimmy as the *Quit* chugged out of Home Bay on her way to Pender Harbour. It was a strange sensation to be all alone on the island with two young boys. As we all sat around the breakfast table, I stressed the need for them to be very cautious in their adventures. "Try to be watchful at all times, fellas, and take action a lot slower and more carefully than you normally would. We are now on our own."

Just before dusk we heard and saw the *Quit* enter Home Bay, and we all ran down to the dock for news of Jenny. Jimmy was alone. I asked him if he would come up to the house for dinner. "Sure, be glad to," he replied. "Jenny was pretty weak by the time we made it to the hospital, and her attacks were more severe." They had kept her in the hospital and recommended she stay. The doctor was fearful of Jenny living so far away from help, and had recommended they move into a hospital cottage so she could be near help.

"Oh Jimmy, we would really hate to lose you two!" I said. "But if her health is at risk, we do understand."

A few days later Jimmy returned to Pender Harbour, taking a few of his and Jenny's belongings. We quietly watched him leave. To lose great friends cast a shadow over us, and now we were alone. We had lost our mentors. It would take a bit of adjusting to get used to being on our own. Roger especially missed Jimmy, because Jimmy's special way of showing Roger the ropes of island life was gone. Often Roger would correct Evan's way of doing a project, saying, "Jimmy said to do it this way." Jenny had been a joy to me—a gentle lady yet able to cope with primitive surroundings and turn adversities into adventures.

The island would now require a caretaker, year round or at least when we were not aboard. The boys and I rowed over to Rouse Bay to visit the Phillips family and to use their telephone. We called Ed in Seattle for advice. Talking it over, we decided to advertise for a caretaker in the Nanaimo, Victoria and Vancouver papers.

The summer days melted away quickly. Late one warm afternoon, while the boys and I were enjoying a swim in the bay, Edward Phillips and his new speedboat glided in. Roger reached the boat as Edward cut the engine, and pulled the boat up on the beach.

"Good to see you, Edward," I greeted him with a wet handshake.

"I wanted to test out my new boat and motor," he replied, "and thought I would bring you this bundle of mail."

I invited him up for tea, but he said he had to get back, as he would be needed for chores.

"I understand, Edward. Give our regards to all your family, and thanks so much for bringing the mail over."

The boys and I waved him on his way.

Back at the house, we opened a large pouch full of letters

and spread them out on the kitchen table. Roger looked through them and noticed that most were from Canada. "Can I have the stamps, Mom, for my collection?"

"Sure, why not? Get some scissors and cut them out if you like."

The first letter was from Nanaimo. It read: "I respectfully am replying to your advertisement I see in the *Free Press* for a caretaker. I am a retired pensioner age 60 years. Let me know all the particulars and what wages you pay. Have you a house there, as I have a wife? If not, I could live up there and let my wife stay here in Nanaimo as we have a house here. So I will be very thankful if you will let me know these things."

Another applicant from Nanaimo wanted to know: "What are the accommodations on the island? Any other people living there. The duties you would expect, and what reimbursement is offered. I receive an old age pension of $40 only. My wife is not eligible as yet for a pension. My wife and I are both clean and tidy, in and out of the house, and like outdoor life, both good gardeners."

A longer one had come from White Rock, BC.

On Tuesday July 19 my daughter and I took a trip up coast by bus to see the island. However, when we arrived at Madeira Park, Pender Harbour, we were informed by an old timer in the district that there was no water taxi as it had gone out of business. We were told by the same fellow that there was no accommodations for us to stay the night at a reasonable rate. As it was 7 p.m. we took his advice and went on to Powell River. When we arrived in Powell River we went to the Canadian Legion. There we saw a Mr. Schouan, a very kindly man who gave us a meal and accommodations for the night, as I did not have enough money to do so.

After making inquiries, Mr. Schouan told us it would cost $30 to $40 to take a plane to the island. I certainly could not do that. With the Legion supplying our bus ticket back to Vancouver, as I had a return ticket from White Rock to Vancouver, also they gave us a bit of money for meals. Our fares cost $17.47 and I can hardly afford this out of my pension. I am not complaining, just understand that I am very disappointed in not being able to see the island, as I am extremely interested in your offer. If some other arrangement can be made for my getting there I would gladly go.

A retired railway worker from Salt Spring Island figured that "a man who can work and look after a section of railway for twenty-five years can be considered reliable." And an ex-farmer in Vancouver wrote:

I am an ex-general mixed farmer, healthy and active, in search of a good farm and which I could manage on a working share basis. I have a little funds, just a few hundred dollars and a Chesapeake Bay dog and a car, enough to help on the grub requirements. If there you have enough funds to invest in seed and a foundation stock of two good cows, one sow and some poultry, as well as secure me for my efforts over a period of five years, I might consider contracting myself with a view to more adequate rewards in the long run.

Just as I reached for another envelope, Roger sighed, "I'm hungry."

"OK," I replied. "What would you like?"

Smartly, Roger answered, "A hamburger, french fries and a chocolate malted."

"How about some bully beef and mashed potatoes and greens?"

We put our lunch on a tray and enjoyed it out on the front verandah in the noonday sun. After lunch the boys went down to the shore for a bit of beachcombing and I returned to the kitchen table to read a few more inquiries.

"I am a medical intern," the next letter began, "and at present not working. I am forty years old and with good character and background. I do not use liquor or smoke, and am very neat in appearance, and of a very quiet disposition."

I placed the letter on top of the others and got up to light the kerosene lantern, stoke the cook stove with a heavy piece of fir bark, then take the tea kettle out to the back porch and fill it from a huge bucket of spring water. As the tea water came to a boil, I heard scuffling outside on the back porch where the boys were spreading out their beach loot. We munched cookies and drank tea while opening yet more letters.

A man from Nanaimo was offering the services of his brother, and one from a retired telephone worker who was "looking for something to do." Another was from a forty-nine-year-old farmer looking for a change, and the writer of the last letter I opened, from Vancouver, wondered: "How many acres are to be maintained and also is it a yearly job or just summertime? Where is this island located, what is its name, also the wages you expect to pay?"

I gathered up the opened and unopened letters and set them all aside for later.

After breakfast the following morning, the boys and I trudged down to weed and water Jenny's garden near the orchard. At one corner of the garden was a sunken water well, into which we dipped a large bucket on a rope.

"Hey, Roger, quit hitting me with water," squealed Evan.

"Come on, Roger," I said. "Let's get the water on the plants and leave your brother alone."

Suddenly we noticed a small group of crisply dressed people peering at us over the garden fence. Our own well-worn duds were quite grimy, washed mainly in the salt chuck with a scrubbing board, and occasionally in our gasoline washing machine, which ran only on its own terms.

The first to address us was a tall middle-aged man dressed in spotless yachting attire. "I'm James Brown from Anacortes, Washington," he said, "and these are a few friends." He introduced them to us. "We hope you don't mind us hiking over your island. We have been out on our boats for several days and appreciate stretching our sea legs. What a grand garden you have!"

"My boys and I are just taking care of it. The lady who planted the garden is quite ill, and is unable to enjoy it." I bent down and pulled a few small carrots, beets, and a head or two of lettuce and cabbage while I answered their questions: Do you live here? How long have you been here? Are you lonesome? What do the boys do for an education? They responded to all of my answers with *Oh*s and *Ah*s.

We clambered over the fence to show the boaters the orchard. One of the older men remarked, "These are pretty ancient fruit trees. I wonder what varieties they are?" He pointed to an English walnut tree with his walking stick and shouted, "I have never come across such a large walnut tree in my born days."

While he was admiring the tree, a pileated woodpecker was busy with his chisel-like bill, burrowing out insects for his brunch, and there was a call of "Quick, George, take a picture of the bird."

Green-shelled walnuts scattered on the ground attracted a small boy, who exclaimed, "Gee, Dad, I didn't know walnuts grew like this." He pierced the green outer shell and found the inside hull beneath the shell. He took out his small pocket knife and cut away the shell to find a small, brown, tightly formed nut. As soon as he put the nut in his mouth, he spat it out. "It's bitter!" he yelled.

I tried to explain that the nut needs time to mature to be eaten. "Many times when we hike up to the hills we find open walnut shells scattered about," I told him. "The crows and ravens take them up high and drop the nuts on the rocks below to open them for a treat.

"Would you folks like a few apples?" I asked. "There are way too many here for us." Two of the boat ladies thanked me, commenting that "an apple crisp would be wonderful."

Spring lambs were bouncing about among the trees with their elders. As we shook the lower branches of the apple trees, the sheep ran to gobble the fallen apples with gusto. We had to scurry to gather them up ahead of the sheep.

One of the small children was fascinated by a newborn lamb that had been abandoned by its mother. We had taken over and we were bottle-feeding the young one. The girl held the nursing bottle for the hungry lamb, which wiggled its tiny tail in appreciation while the child tittered and giggled with glee. Roger held the little girl astride a mature ewe and gave her a bit of a ride around the orchard. As the boaters were about to leave, one of the older boys asked if Roger and Evan would like to come sailing with them in the morning. They certainly did! I agreed, and they said they would pick up the boys around seven in the morning.

I thanked them, but had to ask whether they had checked their tide book. This bay in front of the house goes completely dry at low tide," I said. "It dries out to that large reef in the centre of the bay." I explained that a sailboat with a deep keel would have difficulties navigating through except at high tide. "I believe it would be best if my boys walked over to Deep Bay where you are anchored," I said.

Then I asked, "Could we tempt you with a drink of our homemade root beer?" At this suggestion, Roger ran down to the spring with some of the boat youngsters and brought up a pail full of bottles.

"I remember seeing these same type of bottles when I was a kid," one of the older ladies noted.

"You should see some of the strange bottles we have in the basement under the house," Roger told her. He jumped up, dug out a bottle and brought it up for inspection. The bottles were about a pint in size, with metric numbers marked on the sides. He told everyone what Jimmy had said: that they had floated in after a big winter storm, and had been filled with embalming fluid. At this revelation many *Oh*s and *Ah*s were heard. One of the fellows took a bottle in his hand for inspection. Turning it around, he said, "Quite an interesting piece of glass. Looks old all right—it has a purple tinge to it. Amazing that it reached the island."

They thanked us for a wonderful visit and the refreshing root beer, and promised to be back in the morning.

As the shrouds of night were scattered by the first morning light through my bedroom window, I could hear Roger stir out of his bed upstairs. I could barely get dressed for the day before the boys were outdoors and washed up for breakfast.

Evan shouted from the back porch, "Can I take my fins and goggles with me?"

"We are going sailing, not swimming, dummy," Roger answered.

"Don't forget to take your life jackets with you, and wear them at all times on the boat. Be very careful. Now Roger, take care of your brother. He hasn't been on a sailboat before."

"Don't worry, Mom, I'll watch out for him." They devoured a big breakfast and were off to Deep Bay for an adventurous day on the sea.

After they left, I set a new batch of whole wheat bread, and went out to the front verandah with an interesting book. I was deep into the third chapter when I heard the roar of an outboard engine. Looking out over Home Bay, I saw a speedboat approaching the beach. It slowed and stopped, and two men disembarked and began to unload heavy leather suitcases. I put down my book and walked down the path to meet them.

One man was tall and lanky, and wearing shiny black leather shoes, which were getting soaked in the salt chuck. He swaggered as he approached me and eyed me contemptuously. I greeted him with reluctance.

"Where is the owner of the island?" he demanded. "I have come to be caretaker of this estate and I need to see him immediately."

Just as I was about to tell him to get back on the boat, the skipper of the speedboat leaped back in and took off before I could stop him. So I straightened up to my full five feet and said, "My husband and I are owners of this island, and it is an isolated, rugged coastal retreat, far from being an estate."

Oblivious to my remark, he continued. He had been accustomed to gracious country living, he said, and hoped this would meet his demands. He hoped we served wholesome, nutritious meals filled with vitamins, as he considered his body to be his temple.

I interrupted this incorrigible male with, "How did you find out we needed a caretaker?"

He had contacted the newspaper directly and they had given him the information he needed. "I do not believe in putting things off," he announced.

No way was this fellow going to spoil our summer holiday. My foremost thought was, how do I send him packing in a hurry?

With joy I noticed that the sailboat with the boys aboard was gliding carefully into the bay with the high tide. I untied the dinghy and rowed out to pick them up and thank their hosts. They graciously said Roger and Evan were great sailors and a pleasure to have aboard. We waved farewell as the boys shouted about how much fun they had had. Evan boasted that he had been allowed to steer the boat, and Roger told me how he had worked the sails. They both sputtered with excitement about how we needed a sailboat too.

"Sounds like you two had a real adventure," I replied.

"Yeah, Mom, we rounded the south end of Texada, and sailed the Malaspina Channel and tacked back and forth. The wind really picks up the boat and takes it along where it wants."

When we got to shore, Roger noticed the suitcases on the beach. "Whose are these?" he asked.

"Mine," the stranger answered. Roger looked at him quizzically.

Leaving the stranger's baggage on the beach, we all made our way up the path to the house. I asked the fellow to wait for us a minute while the boys and I went down to the spring for fresh drinking water. This gave us a chance to discuss how we would rid ourselves of our unwanted guest. When we caught sight of a small tugboat slowly pulling a long tow of logs, presto! We had our solution. "Let's give him a real coastal adventure," I squealed.

We rushed back to the house and told the man to follow us to the beach. Roger readied the boat and I threw in his luggage and told him to jump into the boat, as we were going to show him around the island. He muttered something while we rowed the boat as hard as we could to catch the tug.

As we approached the tail end of the log tow, I yelled at our visitor to jump on the end of the boom and get ready to tie us on. He did so, but instead of throwing him the rope from the boat, I tossed his luggage onto the logs after him. And that was the end of him. We rowed merrily away from the log boom and headed back to our island.

When a situation becomes impossible in an isolated region, with no means of communication or transportation, one must sometimes take desperate measures, I told myself to ease my uneasy conscience. In the days following I wondered about the astonishment of the tugboat crew when they discovered a stowaway on the end of their log boom. A few weeks later, I received a very unflattering postcard from the unwelcome visitor. I do hope he eventually found a way of life to his liking.

The next day I wrote a letter to Ed asking him to carefully check out anyone who applied for the caretaking position, before they made the trip to the island. I also wrote a bit of what happened to the last would-be caretaker. It was mail day on Lasqueti, so we decided to run the letter over in the boat so it would reach Ed as soon as possible. When we arrived on the beach at Rouse Bay, we found Edward Phillips and a middle-aged man standing nearby. He approached our boat and vigorously gave us a hand in anchoring it out. Edward introduced us to Mr. Powell, a prospective caretaker for Jedediah. Oh no, I thought, not another. He stood straight and tall, his hands were large and deeply creased, and when he spoke, his eyes searched directly into mine. "I arrived on Lasqueti yesterday and met Mr. Lewis," he said, "who kindly put me up for the night in his home. In the morning he drove me in his truck to the Phillipses'. They believed you might come for your weekly mail today and give me a chance to meet up with you."

"You have had quite a trip," I replied. "It's heartwarming to know that folks here on the island are so hospitable to strangers." As we walked up the path to the Phillips home, I offered to take him back to Jedediah that evening, so he could take a look at the island and we could decide if he was the right person to take care of Jedediah.

We were cheerfully greeted by Evadne, who was busy working in her front garden. "Come on inside for a cool drink," she offered. Evadne's mother and Diane had heard us approach and had glasses full of blackberry juice ready for everyone. We joined her in the parlour, where she was busily working on her needlepoint. Edward asked Diane if she would play us a bit of a tune on the piano. "Oh, Edward," she said, "I don't play that well for visitors to suffer with." But we all coaxed her and she shyly began to play a lovely piece of music that filled the room and moved outdoors to put shame to the birds. When Diane finished her playing, the day was turning to dusk and I suggested we head back to Jedediah. We picked up our mail, headed down to the beach and boarded the boat. Mr. Powell put the oars into the locks and pulled them heartily through the water until we reached Home Bay, then Roger took the oars and guided the boat through the reefs to Jimmy's dock.

"What a peaceful and tranquil place," Mr. Powell said when we arrived.

"Yes," I replied, "most of the time, except early in the morning when Old Red, the rooster, begins his day and then the ravens and crows join in the chorus. In the evening we have the crickets, owls and frogs to keep us company." I showed Mr. Powell to an upstairs bedroom for his stay. After a light snack we turned in.

Mr. Powell was first to reach the kitchen the next morning. He started the wood stove and had the coffee pot perking when I greeted him with a sleepy "Good morning." I put on a pan for porridge. Then I asked Mr. Powell—or Bill, as he preferred, "How did you know about the caretaking job on Jedediah?"

"I have a friend who works at the *Nanaimo Free Press*," he answered, and he called me about the ad; he thought I would be interested. I made plans to come and see you."

After breakfast we all walked to the orchard, where two

huge rams were staring at each other. They backed up a few paces, then with great speed they started to run toward each other. What a crash! The sound and fury of their horns and skulls meeting was deafening. Then they backed up again and had another go at it. "It often happens this time of year," Bill explained to the boys, "Soon it will be mating season. They are testing each other out."

"You boys take Bill around and show him Boom Bay and Deep Bay," I suggested, "and if you have any energy left, go to Long Bay and to the top of the mountain. I'll stay in the garden for a while and get a few things for lunch."

As I prepared lunch I heard the sound of a speedboat. It was Art Ryan. I met him on the beach and he held up the back quarter of a deer, all dressed out ready for the pan or the canning jars. The boys and Bill had also heard Art's boat and were soon on the beach to admire the bounty.

I introduced Bill and Art.

"What a great part of the world this is. Do you live near here?" Bill asked.

"I'm from Bull Island, the next closest rock to Jedediah. I am logging over there and have a crew of ten kids and a wife with me."

"I can see you are a busy man," Bill replied. "We might become good neighbours, as I am certain I would like to caretake Jedediah, if that is OK by the Mattice family."

"It appears you might be the fellow we need," I remarked. "At least we'll give it a try and see how it works out for both of us." Bill said he needed to get back to Nanaimo to pack up a few belongings and take care of renting out his house. Art offered to take him over to Anderson Bay on Lasqueti, then he could get a ride on the main road to False Bay, and from there take a water taxi to French Creek. Bill went home that day.

Several mornings later, we were awakened by the sound of a

speedboat in the bay. I dressed quickly and ran down to greet the visitors. A plump fortyish lady attempted to step over the side of the boat and as it tipped a bit, she screamed, "Vic!" A heavy, muscular fellow came to her rescue, giving her a hand to step down on a large, flat rock. Her gumboots slipped on the half-submerged rock and down she went. We heard a few expletives as she righted herself and stood up to her full height, soaking wet.

I offered my hand to her and said, "Come up to the house and dry off a bit. I have a change of clothes for you."

"No," she said, "I'm OK. It isn't the first time I have been soaked in the salt chuck." She tossed her long dark hair about and announced, "I'm Mildred Tucker. My mother Eva Tucker owns and operates a lumber mill on Lasqueti, and this is Vic Looke, he runs the lumber mill for my mother. We have come to talk to you about your timber on Jedediah."

While Mildred and I were talking Vic tied the speedboat to a float we had fastened together. I invited them up to the house for a cup of coffee. I was quite curious about their prospective offer on the timber. Word had travelled around Lasqueti that I was a well-to-do American with no knowledge of coastal life, especially the value of timber. But in fact, my stepfather had been an old-time gyppo logger, and I grew up in logging camps and lumber mills. I was getting my jollies by keeping this knowledge to myself as I led them down the orchard path into some deep virgin stands of fine timber. "See, these trees are beyond their prime," Vic declared. "They are conky and twisted with the wind, and will be difficult to get off the island." I listened as he continued to denigrate the quality and value of the trees. He stood straight and pulled vigorously on his broad suspender straps as he announced, "Looks like this timber is worth about eight dollars a thousand."

I looked squarely at Vic and said, "I am aware of the state of these trees, and I have lived through the destruction of huge swaths of virgin timber on the Olympic Peninsula in Washington state, that have been sacrificed for the almighty dollar. I am not interested in trashing Jedediah. This stand of timber is staying as it is now and forever. You may have noticed a few trees have been cut in the early 1900s. The lumber was used only to build the house and barns here, and that's enough logging for me." I told him I knew he was in the lumber business and that I applauded his ingenuity in scouting for timber. But, I said, "you can be certain as long as we own Jedediah—or, more correctly, Jedediah owns us—no trees will be sacrificed." On our walk back to the beach, I thanked Mildred and Vic for the visit and welcomed them to return along with their families at any time. They hurriedly boarded their speedboat as the tide receded swiftly from the bay.

At the same moment, we all looked skyward to see a large seaplane circling the bay.

"Maybe it's Dad!" Evan yelled.

"I hope so, Evan," I replied.

"The tide is out too far for the plane to land in the bay," Roger said. "I'll take the rowboat out to meet the plane and bring Dad in."

Float planes are a great convenience for coast people. Without them, large areas of rugged terrain would be completely inaccessible. But debris such as half-sunken logs or undetected reefs give a seaplane pilot nightmares. The engine cut out and I watched as the pontoons glided smoothly over the water. Ed jumped out of the plane, and boxes and bags of supplies followed. Roger helped load the freight from plane to boat, then he pushed the wing of the plane away from the boat so the pilot could take off again.

It was great to be together again. Our little family carried the boxes and bags up the hill to the house. Evan reached into one of the boxes and squealed, "Oh boy, ice cream!"

I looked at Ed and said sadly, "Sure wish we could share a bit of this ice cream with Jenny and Jimmy." Ed asked how Jenny was getting along in the hospital at Pender Harbour. I didn't know. "But I am concerned. Every mail day I look for a note about her condition. We can only hope and pray for the best."

He patted my arm, saying, "We'll hear soon."

After we had unpacked our new supplies and finished our ice cream, Ed said, "Mary, I don't see why we can't sell our business and home in Seattle, and retire here on the island. I know it's the life you want and I could be content here too with plenty of books, my paints and canvases."

"Oh, Ed, do you think it could be possible?" I jumped up from the kitchen table and threw my arms around Ed's neck. "I'm convinced that it's the proper way of life for our boys, too. Let's give it a lot of serious thought. It would be a dream come true for all of us."

"Only one aspect worries me," Ed said. "How about the boys' education?"

"I have talked to Helen Ryan about the possibility of schooling with our two boys and her crew on Bull Island," I said. "She told me that her niece, a former schoolteacher, is willing to stay on to teach our boys and the Ryan youngsters. The niece's husband is working with Art Ryan on the logging operation. If this arrangement is impractical, we could teach our boys with a correspondence course from the school district in Victoria."

Our attention was caught by the distant drone of a plane. Roger and Evan raced down to the beach and pulled our rowboat over the wet sandy, tide flats to where they could float it. Then they boarded it and rowed out to meet the float plane. In a few minutes they returned to the tide flats with two men, and they all began to dig for clams. Roger ran up to the house to tell us they wanted a few clams to take home, and that they had offered to give the boys a ride in their plane.

Ed gave his permission, then told Roger, "In Canada the clams belong to everyone. In the States, the shoreline tide flats usually belong to the upland owners, clams and all." Roger swiftly returned to the beach. The two pilots waved and yelled to check whether it was OK for the boys to go up in their plane. We waved back in the affirmative.

When the boys returned they gave us a full report. The fellows owned a company called Pacific Wings, and they sold planes in Vancouver. They were so pleased with Jedediah, they wanted to bring their wives up the next weekend for a treat. The boys were thrilled at the possibility of yet another plane ride.

A few more glorious summer days passed. Ed and I spent many hours seriously discussing the pros and cons of moving permanently to the island. One day we heard a knock at the back door. We were startled, as usually we hear or see a visitor approach. Ed opened the door cautiously, and there stood two people. The man was about age forty, quite slight of build

Roger and Evan aboard a seaplane over Jedediah, 1950.

with bushy blond hair pushed down by a blue woollen fisherman's cap. Standing beside him was a woman, a bit younger. She was tall, thin and weather-worn. Wisps of thin, light brown hair hung down past her shoulders. Her slight frame was covered with a brown, loosely knit wool sweater. These visitors were definitely not tourists.

The man spoke hesitantly. "We hear you are in need of a caretaker for the island."

"Yes," Ed answered, "we are."

"My name is Lars and my wife's name is Penny."

"We are Ed and Mary, owners of Jedediah," Ed offered.

"We often fish around the island," Lars went on, "and could caretake the place in the off-season from fishing, during late winters especially. We have our own transportation, a thirty-two-foot fishing troller, and we are used to living alone and we don't have children in need of an education."

I invited them into the kitchen for a cup of coffee and a talk. I told them that a fellow had been here around ten days ago, and seemed willing and able to take on the job, but I had not heard from or seen him since. Perhaps he had changed his mind, or become involved with other matters.

"Give us a few days to think the idea over," Ed said, "and see if this fellow shows up. In the meantime where is your fish boat anchored?"

"We have it anchored now in your Deep Bay," Lars answered. "We are tied up to a log boom there."

"We'll walk over tomorrow and talk more about it," Ed replied.

Penny and Lars thanked us for the coffee and chat, and went on their way. The following morning after breakfast, Ed, the boys and I went to the garden to weed and water before we took off for Deep Bay to see Lars and Penny. I pulled some fresh carrots, beets, cabbage and lettuce to take to them on their boat.

"I think it's a great idea to go over to their boat," I told Ed. "As you know, this house on the island is not ready for an award from *House Beautiful*, but it is neat, tidy, and livable. It could be a haven for a trash pile if not taken care of." With burlap bags filled with vegetables, we took off over the trail to Deep Bay in search of Penny and Lars's boat.

We pushed our way through fallen logs and underbrush until we came to the old logging skid road. During the early 1900s, when a bit of timber was logged, this trail of cedar slabs was the easiest route through the woods to get the trees to the water. The fallen trees were skidded over this road, which was greased so that horses or oxen could more easily pull the logs down to the beach. The logs were taken to Boom Bay, near Deep Bay, and the cedar skids were still there after fifty years. As the trail to Deep Bay opened up, we saw Lars and Penny's troller.

Lars noticed us, put his dinghy into the water and rowed toward us.

"Top of the morning to you," Ed greeted him.

"Glad to have you aboard," Lars replied. "It would be best if I took Mary and the boys first in the dinghy, then return for you, Ed."

"You're the captain," Ed called back. "We'll follow orders."

The two boys jumped eagerly into the small boat. I stepped into the middle of the craft carefully to keep it from rolling. We all sat on the centre board seat and Lars dipped his oars swiftly into the still water. Soon we were at the edge of the sturdy wooden fish boat. Penny pushed the skiff away slightly to prevent it from hitting the hull of the troller too hard. Then she tied a small rope to it and fastened it to the fish boat. "Welcome aboard," she said, reaching out to help us board the boat.

We stepped over the edge of the boat to the deck, which was freshly painted a sea blue. The wheelhouse sparkled with a new coat of pale yellow paint. "Come on in and have a bite of lunch with us." Penny beckoned us down into the galley area. Bright, shiny linoleum covered the galley floor. Penny put a tiny tea kettle under the water tap, filled it to the top and placed it on a compact oil-burning stove. Above the small sink were open cupboards with heavy crockery stacked in rows. A narrow strip of wood kept the dishes from tumbling down in a stormy sea. Penny put heavy coffee mugs on the fold-down table in the centre of the galley as Ed and Lars appeared at the galley door. Lars offered Ed a drop of rye before lunch, and Ed declined.

The boys were fascinated by the array of fishing gear hanging on the walls of the wheelhouse. Roger touched the dangling tentacles of a wiggling lure, and Lars held one in his hand and explained. "It's a newfangled lure called a hootchy-kootchy. They come in all combinations of colours—chartreuse with pink dots, cerise and orange, and any mixture of colours you could imagine. Here, Roger, take this one. It might bring you luck."

"Oh thanks, Lars," was Roger's response, as he carefully tucked his new treasure into his shirt pocket.

Lars beckoned them to come below. "I'll show you what powers the boat."

Ed and the boys went below, and we could hear Lars saying, "She's a mighty dependable motor, a 7-horsepower machine that turns at 600 rpm, and pushes the boat to 7 to 8 knots. I keep her in top running order, as she is the throbbing heart and soul of this craft." Penny yelled down to the engine room, "Tea is on." She poured strong black tea for the adults and asked the boys if they would like Cambridge tea.

Evan murmured, "I would like some please."

"You make it like Mom's," Roger chimed in, "only she puts in too much tinned milk and not enough sugar for me."

Penny brought out a pretty painted tin box filled with delicious oatmeal cookies, which we all enjoyed.

By now, dusk was beginning to darken the corners of the bay. We took leave of the boat and thanked Penny and Lars for their hospitality. Ed asked them to come over to the house the next day to make plans to caretake the island for the winter, and they agreed to see us in the morning.

Along the trail back to the house, Ed said, "Looks like they'll make good caretakers. What do you think, Mary?"

"Yes, seems like our best inquiry so far. They do keep their boat very shipshape."

Penny and Lars stayed on Jedediah during the late fall, until just before the Christmas holidays. Their last letter to us, written on December 3, 1951, was filled with sadness and gloom.

I thought I would write you a few lines to let you know how we are and that we are still here on the island, as no doubt you have been wondering if we had moved. We plan on going to Vancouver somewhere around the fifteenth of the month, and will be there for Christmas. We have enjoyed living on the island and have learned a lot about pioneer life. Lars will put the chain saw and outboard motor and keys to the house and shed in the barrel and place it in the thicket of blackberry bushes where Ed had hidden the chain saw. No point in putting them in the attic as they wouldn't be there, someone would steal them. Many mornings we have been awakened by rifle shots in the orchard, but so far have not been able to catch anybody. Lars has chased after them many times.

Lars counted ten dead sheep over by Deep Bay, and we figured whoever shot them had planned on taking a boatload but had to leave them when Lars began chasing them. They certainly don't pay any attention to your No Hunting signs. With so many strangers hunting on the island and shooting from their boats, these people don't seem to realize there's anyone living on the island. About a month ago someone broke into our fish boat at Deep Bay and stole the sounder, anchor and other equipment totalling about seven hundred dollars. Due to that we moved the boat to Bull Island at Art Ryan's A-frame. A week or two later, the A-frame fell over on the boat and smashed the cabin, sinking the boat. Lars hired a tug to tow it to the bay on Cowley's where he worked on it. We now have the boat here in Deep Bay again where Lars has been working on it. As soon as he gets it running, we will leave.

The day the boat sunk, we were all packed to go to town when Dave Cowley came over and told us about the boat. To top it off, our insurance policy on the boat had just run out. So you see we have had our share of bad luck here, yet we enjoyed living here just the same.

I have used some of your canning jars, Mary, to can deer meat and fish. I will return the jars next spring when we begin to fish again.

We have had lots of company here, mostly men. Cowleys come over quite often, also Art Ryan at least once or twice a week. He and Lars have gone hunting on Texada a lot together for deer.

The days are so short now and the house is cold, we practically live in the kitchen near the cooking stove. We have not been able to use the fireplace as the chimney is unsafe. It must be cracked in several places, as the smoke seeps out of the chimney box upstairs and attic. We replaced the stovepipes in the kitchen stove, it sure burns better since.

Well, we had our first snowstorm of the season. It snowed about an inch, and the weather forecast on the radio calls for more snow and gale winds for tonight. I envy those lucky people who have automatic oil heat tonight. We sleep in our eiderdown sleeping bags.

Oh, I must tell you some good news. I found a pearl in an oyster, too bad it was only a tiny one. Well,

Christmas will soon be here and far too soon to suit me.
I haven't baked my cakes yet. Hello to you all and hope
you are all well.

We received their letter in Seattle just a few days before
Christmas. It was a reminder that life is not a bed of roses for
many people who strive to live in an isolated area. One must be
very self-sufficient, capable of coping with isolation and
extremely adept at managing the land, animals and machinery
that make it all possible. After Christmas I wrote to Penny and
Lars to express our regret that they could no longer live on
Jedediah. Ed and I agreed that it seemed impossible to find a
caretaker who was willing to live on the island permanently.
Now the ball was in our court. We must move to Jedediah permanently.

As we discussed our plans, the boys became ecstatic. "Oh
boy, no more school," Roger expressed himself loudly.

"You heard us read Penny's letter," Ed said. "It is not all fun
and games. Island living takes a great deal of planning, putting
up with hardships, and back-breaking labour. Remember, you
have been there only in the summers, when all was cozy and
warm, never during the long, dark, cold and windy winters."

"Jenny and Jimmy lived there all year round," Roger
answered. "Also the homesteaders."

Several months passed before we found a buyer for our
home and nursery business. We spent the time searching war surplus and secondhand stores for sturdy gear and how-to books for
pioneer living. We disposed of our luxury home furnishings and
bric-a-brac. We found an old-time cast-iron cooking stove which
would prove to be a "mother" to us on the island. Our excitement about our new way of life was overwhelming. As soon as
school summer holidays began and the new owners of the business were in charge, we were ready for Jedediah.

We contracted a trucking firm to take our household goods to Vancouver, then hired a barge company to transport everything to Jedediah. Packed in among the household items, tools and machinery were two large Afghan hound dogs, a small grey kitten, plus twelve mature red laying hens. We cleared customs at the Douglas crossing close to Blaine, Washington and we were granted Canadian Landed Immigrant status.

Our departure from the harbour in Vancouver was uneventful. As we passed slowly under the Lions Gate Bridge, the boys were ecstatic. We all found the wheelhouse of the mighty tug inviting. It was equipped with unique and modern navigation instruments, and best of all a massive oil stove with a perky coffee pot secured on its top. A companionway in the wheelhouse led down to the fo'c's'le and bunks. The head (toilet) was down near the engine. A Swedish-made diesel engine pulsated and pulled the barge full of freight at a slow, steady pace. All was smooth sailing across the open waters of the Strait of Georgia.

A slight northerly wind increased as we approached the south end of Texada. I anxiously kept one eye on the antique china cabinet my grandmother had left to me. It was lashed down near the end of the barge with ropes that I could see straining with the rougher water. The boys ran around the outside deck of the tug and Roger snapped a photo every few minutes until his camera ran out of film. The deckhand on the tug, a young fellow of sixteen, chummed with the boys, showing them how to tie boat ropes properly and handle the many other chores necessary to run a tug.

As we turned course from the south end of Texada, the skipper of the tug asked where he should anchor to unload the barge. We could see from the sides of the rocky outcropping that the tide was low. The skipper reached for his tide tables book and noted that high tide would occur early in the morning, around 4:30 or 5:00 a.m. "Where is the best location to put down the anchor for the night?" he asked.

"It will be safe to leave the tug and barge at the entrance to Home Bay," Ed answered. "Rarely does a southeast wind blow up at this time of year, also it will be easy for unloading in the morning." We all settled down for the night aboard the tug. The night was dark, spilling over with sparkling stars. Below us, the water churned with silky black dogfish. The boys pushed pike poles down to stir them up. Phosphorescence glittered on their poles like a Fourth of July sparkler.

The skipper told us that dogfish were prized during the war, when their livers were found to be high in vitamin content and could yield high returns in oil and cash. They were rendered at the "oileries" on the west coast. Dogfish have a hard, gristly sandpaper-like skin instead of scales. "They are used in England in the fish-and-chips shops," he said, "but in Canada, no amount of advertising has succeeded in convincing people to include dogfish steaks in their diet, as yet."

He showed us our bunks for the night and we all crept in wearily.

At dawn, flaming orange streaks of light greeted us. The two Afgan hounds were howling, frantic to reach firm land. The kitten was content sleeping on Evan's bunk, and inside the chicken crate on deck were two huge eggs. "Looks like breakfast is ready," I remarked.

The skipper of the tug gave orders to pull up the anchor and start the engines. We soon sailed into Home Bay, near Jimmy's dock. The crew helped us unload the barge swiftly before the tide could recede, marooning the tug and barge on the tide flats.

"We'll see you again," the skipper said, "during long winter storms, when we tie up near your island and need to give our legs a stretch."

Ed said they were always welcome, and thanked them for bringing us and our belongings to Jedediah. We all waved farewell as the tug made its way out of the bay and back to Vancouver.

All our earthly goods were stacked on the dock, ready to be moved up the path to the house. This would take a week of struggling with crates, boxes and sacks. First the new antique wood-burning stove had to be disassembled and hauled up to the house in small pieces. We used barrows and rollers made of small round logs to move heavy objects up the hill. We found that the old kitchen stove was unsafe—the firebox had rusted out along with the metal chimney. We soon had the new "mother" stove in working order.

Finally the day arrived when all the freight was packed away. Now we could get on with making improvements, before winter approached. Ed installed our water system in the house. Running water pumped up from the spring by the action of the ram jet was a miracle. We built a new two-seater outhouse from boards we scrounged from the beach at low tide, as the old outhouse was dilapidated beyond repair.

Wonderful summer weeks flashed by, and each new day brought new challenges to conquer. Our very existence depended on our ingenuity and our willingness to meet head-on any projects or problems. At times, critters like raccoons, crows, mink and weasels seemed to get the best of the fruit and vegetable crops, along with the occasional feast of a chicken, turkey or guinea fowl to round out their menu.

Tuesdays were mail days on Lasqueti Island. Domville, the water taxi fellow, brought the mail over from Parksville and it was sorted out and placed at individual mailboxes along the main road on Lasqueti. We had a mailbox at the end of the main road, at Squitty Bay.

One day Ed awoke early and routed Roger out of bed with the suggestion that they go fishing and get the mail at Squitty Bay. They left for Lasqueti quickly after breakfast. Evan and I had a leisurely breakfast, but he was a bit disappointed he had missed the mail boat.

"What would you like to do today?" I asked.

He replied, "I'd like to make a better chicken coop and better place for the chickens to lay their eggs, Mom."

"OK, we'll finish the house chores, then go out and see what we can scrounge up for lumber. We have a bunch of nails, hammers and saws in the work shed so we can get at it." Evan held up the rough boards so I could measure and cut out nesting boxes for the hens. We were getting along well with three boxes in place and a fourth in progress, when Ed walked up and greeted us. He looked very distressed. "What's up?" I asked.

He handed me an envelope and I opened it. It contained a notice that the fellow who had bought our business in Seattle could not make a go of it and was unable to make payments on his contract to us. We sadly and thoughtfully walked back to the house. Now that we had found our Shangri-La, we might have to go back to rescue a faltering business in the city.

Ed suggested that it would be best if he went back alone, checked out what was happening and tried to get the fellow back on the right track. The next morning after mail day, the sea was calm and the day bright and sunny with only a few feathers of cloud in the sky. It was a good day to go across to Secret Cove on the mainland, where Ed could catch a bus to Vancouver, then on to Seattle.

Secret Cove, on the Sunshine Coast, was only seven miles from Jedediah. But it could be a treacherous crossing, as it is open water from the south end of Texada to Vancouver harbour. Often a southeastern wind will whip up quickly, and there are no sheltering bays in which to escape a storm. We all boarded our sixteen-foot inboard motor boat. I had packed food and water and extra gas for the motor. Jimmy had warned me never to go out of the bay for any distance without extra supplies. A fog or storm may come up suddenly and you might need to "hole up" for a while.

Just as we rounded the south end of Texada, shooting geysers of spray punctured the calm water before us. A pod of killer whales were leaping out of the water, standing on their tails, then flopping down on the surface. The whales rose three or four times then they sounded below the water and stayed for several minutes. It was a spectacular sight—at times we could almost touch them. Our only fear was that their gymnastic feats would upset our small craft.

The whales rose again, moved away at high speed and were soon clear of us. Evan spoke first. "I wasn't scared," he said. Roger laughed nervously and said he wasn't scared either. The remainder of the trip was uneventful. At Secret Cove, we sadly said our goodbyes to Ed.

Chapter

3

THE TIDE WAS HIGH WHEN WE RETURNED TO Home Bay. Roger tied our inboard motor boat to Jimmy's dock, and we walked up to the house slowly.

Darkness seeped in around the corners of the kitchen. It seemed so empty and lonely without Ed. Yet there's never much time for sad thoughts when young boys are yelling that they are hungry. The new kitchen stove sparked up and got the kettles bubbling quickly. To cheer us, I tuned in the battery radio and we enjoyed a thriller story before going to bed.

The following morning after chores, the boys asked if they could go beachcombing. "Good idea," was my answer.

The tide in the bay was rapidly receding. I watched them skirt around the edge of the tideline in search of any bounty that may have floated in on the high tide. Many times one shoe (never a pair), brooms, buckets, ropes and sometimes a dinghy that had been carelessly tied behind a pleasure boat and gone adrift, and other treasures. They pulled and tugged their finds to high ground for inspection.

The days of summer sped by. Each week we would row over to Rouse Bay on Lasqueti Island and pick up our letter from Ed. After several weeks we received a very discouraging letter, telling us that the person who was buying our business could not handle the task. We would have to move back to Seattle, try to bring back the business, then sell it again.

I decided to phone Ed from the Phillips home, and ask to stay on the island a bit longer, at least another month. We could be back by the first of September, I said, when the boys would be ready for school. Ed agreed reluctantly. Finding a new caretaker for Jedediah on such short notice was impossible. On my way back from the Phillipses we stopped in for a visit with the Ryan family. As we rowed into the bay at Bull Island, we found Art, Sidney and Barbara painting the *Montana*, their fish boat. The boys and I jumped out of the boat and tied it on a long line to a large beached log.

"Go in and have a cup of coffee with Helen and the rest of the crew," Art yelled. "They need cheering up." Evan and Roger stayed down at the beach to watch the painting. I found Helen in the kitchen of the float house, making a trail through with a stiff broom, sweeping away odds and ends of kids, cats, sticks and stones. When she saw me she dropped her broom, pulled a chair up to the table and said, "Sit down and share a cup of coffee with me. Beverley and Colleen made some great cookies early this morning; we'll sample them." I shared my bad news with Helen. "Oh, Mary," she said, "We'll sure hate to see you go back to town. It's been so much fun having you near us."

I agreed. "It seems we were just settling in when this sad news arrived."

Art came into the kitchen for a cup of coffee, which he sipped as he walked about the room and watched out the window, checking on the progress of the paint job.

"Art," Helen said, "Mary and her family have to go back to Seattle for a while. Do you think we could keep a watch on Jedediah for them?"

"Sure," said Art. He explained it wouldn't be a problem for

Eight of the Ryan children (left to right): Linda, Theresa, Irene,
Valerie, Arthur, Sharon, Karen and Colleen, 1960s.

them, as they were so close to Jedediah, and he fished and hunted around the area all the time. "Mary," he continued, "I have a
confession to make. It wasn't an unfortunate accident that my
A-frame fell on your last caretaker's boat. It was a method of getting rid of a very unsavoury fellow. Expensive pieces of logging
equipment disappeared while he was around, also people on
Lasqueti started missing machinery and tools. Sometimes out in
these remote regions we have to do strange things to keep law
and order, giving out our own justice."

I wasn't too surprised. Quite a few of our supplies had also
gone missing.

The boat painters piled into the kitchen and the newly
baked cookies soon disappeared. Even little Arthur came out
from under the kitchen stove and devoured the last cookie.

"Well, fellows," I said at last, "we'd better get back to
Jedediah and start to get organized for leaving." The little ones

hugged us and pleaded with us not to leave.

Helen threw her arms around me and said, "Now don't forget to write to us often and promise to come back soon." Art shook my hand. "Don't worry about the island," he said. "It's been here for thousands of years and it's not going anywhere."

The boys and I rowed out of the bay slowly and sadly. Over the next few days we packed up our supplies and gear, took them out into the woods and buried them carefully inside fallen hollow logs and stumps. We took our chain saw, generator, boats and engines over to Bull Island for safekeeping. Two happy Afghan hounds were added to the crew there.

Reluctantly we left for Seattle. Roger and Evan enrolled in school. Ed and I took over the business and began to revive it. What with the stress and anxiety, I became ill with rheumatic fever and spent several weeks in hospital. My physician ordered me not to return to the business. I longed to be back on Jedediah, where I knew I would recover.

As spring arrived and the boys got ready for their school holidays, I got ready too. We packed our belongings and returned to Jedediah. From Seattle we took passage to Victoria on the grand old lady *Marguerite* and stayed at the magnificent Empress Hotel for a few days. While we were there, I called on the offices of the Ministry of Education to find out how to conduct home schooling.

We took a bus from Victoria to Nanaimo, where we checked into the Malaspina Hotel. Then we began to search for a boat to take us and our supplies to Jedediah. It was the beginning of the salmon fishing season and many boats had already left the docks. We were lucky to find a troller that was headed our way and willing to take us aboard.

The boys and I were anxious to return to Jedediah, and the skipper was anxious to get up north. Trollers are the most independent of fishermen. If a man or woman (there are a few) can rustle up a boat, some fishing gear and lots of endurance, he or she can make a decent living. This time we didn't overload the boat. We took only a few groceries, a new battery, vegetable seeds and fishing tackle.

When the fisherman informed us he was ready to leave, Roger untied the lines and the skipper started the engine. We were slowly cruising between Newcastle Island and Nanaimo Harbour when Evan became interested in the gurdies and fish lines, hung up hopefully during fishing season and ready for the fish. The skipper's calloused and scarred hands turned one of the gurdy handles so Evan could understand how it worked. "Maybe you'll be a fisherman someday, fella," the skipper commented.

"I don't know for sure," was Evan's reply.

"To be a highliner at this game," he said, "you have to pick the right boat, gear and lures and work your gear at the right depths, sometimes slower or faster with the pull of the oars or engines, keeping an eye on the sea and the wind, watching the lines and not forgetting about a possible storm on the horizon. All the while you have to keep tabs on the tides. When the fish are running we might have to stay alert eighteen to twenty hours or more at a stretch."

Evan asked about the bells that were attached to the trolling lines.

"When they ring you know a fish has taken your line—it's a sorta wake-up call," was our skipper's reply.

"How many poles and lines do you usually have out at a time?" Roger asked.

"At the most I put out twelve trolling lines, trailing astern. Two main poles reach out from the midsection of the boat and two bowlines."

Before dusk we reached Home Bay on Jedediah. The tide was out, so the fisherman let us off on a large rock outcropping near Sandy Beach. We thanked him for the trip and paid him for his trouble.

We left our gear on the rocks above the high tide mark and walked over the sandy, wet tidewater to Jimmy's dock. Darkness was on us. We crept up the hill to the house, walked in and tumbled into bed.

The warmth of the morning sun through the window encouraged us to start a new day and begin our island life, without Ed and without Jenny and Jimmy.

The house was ship-shape. The Ryans had done a fine job for us. After breakfast, we heard Art's boat in the bay. He was towing our two smaller boats behind his. We all rushed down to greet him and take care of the boats.

Codfish Bay, one of the many small, beautiful spots on the coastline of Jedediah.

"I thought I noticed a troller going by late yesterday," he said, "and thought it might be you, as the boat turned into the bay. So I thought I would take a look and see."

I asked after Helen and the young ones.

"All's well with us," he reported. "We had a mild winter and I was able to sell all my logs, and the kids are full of hell and healthy. Helen is busy as ever, she is starting to dig in the garden as it's been a warm spring. The young ones have been planting an early garden on their own already."

"Come on up for a cup of coffee, Art."

"I'd like to, Mary, but I have some fellows stopping by about some of my logging machinery and I have to get back soon."

"Thanks, Art," I said gratefully. "Looks like all is well around here and everything in place after a winter of no one in the house. I'll be over in a day or two and pick up the rest of the gear we left with you."

"See you soon," Art called as he sped out of the bay in his boat.

Roger took the rowboat out to where we had left our supplies the evening before. He brought it all to the dock and we all pitched in and hauled the gear up to the house.

We soon fell into a routine of early morning school study, followed by survival chores such as gathering wood, bringing in water and digging the ground in preparation for a vegetable garden. Afternoons and evenings were filled with necessary repairs to our small boats and improvements on our outbuildings: chicken houses, sheep sheds and the barn. Our days were never dull. They were busy with all the interesting chores that sustained us on Jedediah.

Our sixteen-foot boat had a Briggs and Stratton inboard engine which needed attention quite often. I cleaned the spark plugs and set the points every few weeks. Every five or six months I tore apart the engine and rebuilt it. If too much time passed and the engine needed an overhaul, I would put more oil in it until I had time to repair it. Our "putt-putt" was our lifeline and had to be in working order at all times.

The woodpile was a constant concern. All summer we must gather and stack the wood so it would have time to dry for heavy winter use. The storms of winter had broken large limbs from the evergreens, and with a Swede saw we cut them into lengths that would fit the kitchen stove. Old fallen limbs from the orchard were a treasure. These were stacked to dry in the old barn.

Water supply was another continuing concern. Every morning we started the ram jet down at the spring, and if it was temperamental, as it often was, we would bring buckets of water up to the house for drinking and cooking. We saved rainwater in a barrel under the eaves and used this water for washing dishes, clothes and ourselves.

Our late evenings were spent reading, playing cards or working on individual projects—knitting, teasing wool, carving miniature animals or whatever. We used kerosene lanterns for light at first, and then found Aladdin lanterns, which burned much brighter than ordinary kerosene lanterns.

Our summer sped by, we were so engrossed in our daily chores. Maintaining our garden, building the woodpile for winter, repairing engines, harvesting, pickling, canning and storing our food for winter gave us little spare time. Tourists, yachtsmen and local visitors occasionally broke the routines for us, and brought welcome, fun-filled diversions. At low tides, we went beachcombing, dug for clams or just enjoyed the tidal pools. High tides were for swimming and diving off rock outcroppings.

Our main source of food and fun was fishing. On calm, sunny days we would go out in the small rowboat just exploring the other islands and fishing when we felt like it. Often we would row around to our bays and visit yachts and sailboat people. We were amazed how many were from places on the other side of the world from us. They would trade stories of their adventures and ask us about our life on Jedediah. We made many lifelong friends during these encounters.

Our Indian summer gave way to cooler evenings and shorter days. We began to feel the change in the season. Our kitchen stove and fireplace were bringing cozy warmth, and we found ourselves spending more time indoors on schoolwork and reading.

Winter brought peaceful solitude and frequent welcome visits from our neighbours from nearby islands and the mainland. Wintertime gave islanders a chance to spend time enjoying each other's company. The summers were too busy with chores, guests and tourists from all corners of the world—sometimes too many to be appreciated. But in winter, at the sound of a motorboat or the sight of a sail or oars dipping into the water, everyone would rush down to the beach to meet the visitors, and help them tie up their boat or moor it out in a safe tidal area. The table was always set quickly with treats. Greetings and local gossip were exchanged along with current neighbourhood events. These great visits kept us all safe from the dreaded "cabin fever."

One early February day during the annual herring run in the Strait of Georgia, we visited the fish packer's floating barge. The barge, anchored in Rouse Bay on Lasqueti Island, served the fishermen by buying their catch out on the fishing grounds and supplying them with ice, perishable vegetables, fruits and fresh meat along with bakery goods. For us it was a treasure trove of tinned and fresh milk, butter, fresh produce and other food supplies, and we always enjoyed listening and watching the activities of the fish buyers and fishermen. If we were having poor luck in catching fish, we could always buy a fresh one.

This day, on our way home with our bounty of fresh food, we noticed a large flock of seabirds. Among them were some puffy butterball birds, called buffleheads. Some had shiny black feathers on their backs. The backs of their heads were iridescent, showing purple, red and green with sides of dark brownish-grey. The undersides of the birds were a dark brownish white. Buffleheads wintered with us, but in April and May they migrated to breeding grounds and we lost them until fall. These were busy on nearby rock outcroppings, opening small mussels.

Swimming with the buffleheads were shovellers. We

watched them straining out grasses and small sea creatures with their spoon bills. The male is outstanding in full plumage with a bright green head, white breast and a reddish abdomen. The female is a drab, light brown color. Her less splendid plumage is compensated for by the luxury of two husbands. After she has paired up amiably with one male, the second husband comes along. He is usually a year-old drake with incomplete plumage, who has found that the young females of his generation have gone off by themselves and do not intend to mate until the next season. Quite a handy arrangement for some of us up-island ladies! Who said ducks are dumb?

We watched two long, thin minks run along the sandy beach. We startled them and they disappeared in the nearby beach brush. A few sheep grazed on beached seaweed. They require and savour the salts and minerals in the seaweed. When we got back, Roger and I began to haul up our fresh groceries. As Evan fumbled in the bags for goodies, Roger yelled, "Get busy and help load these bags up to the house!" I left them to pack up the groceries, took a load up to the house and started to prepare a late lunch.

From the front verandah I saw Cathy and David Cowley step out of their boat, with their gumboots deep in the tidal water. I waved them welcome, and yelled, "Come up for lunch."

The Cowleys and my boys sat around the kitchen table while I cooked a few pork chops (from the fish barge), boiled a pot of potatoes and cut up some winter storage kohlrabi and carrots. Cookies and tea finished the meal. The Cowleys gave us the local news of Lasqueti. This was in the mid-1950s, when loggers were abroad on Lasqueti, taking booms and booms of logs away to the mills. Some were trespassing on each other's property and many a scuffle resulted. New people were beginning to arrive to claim or buy logged-off lands for summer cottages or retirement homes. David said he would sell when the price suited him, and

Cathy remarked that they would need to move to town when their young ones grew up, as the school on Lasqueti only went up to the sixth grade.

The winter light was fading. Cathy and David boarded their small speedboat and were gone, back to Anderson Bay on the south end of Lasqueti.

Winters were filled with great visits from the Ryan family—good fun for the boys and me, as the little ones invaded the crannies of the old house and gardens.

Other times the boys and I would go to Pender Harbour for supplies. We would cross the Sabine Channel and Malaspina Strait at the same time as the Dougan and Cox families, who operated a prosperous logging show on the south end of Texada. The camp bustled with their forestry operations—bunkhouses, family homes and cook houses brought in by barge—but it was totally isolated from the settled north end of Texada, which had a grocery store, gas station, hotel and hardware store. We would carefully choose a quiet, calm, cloudless day to cross to Pender Harbour, but unpredictable squalls come up quickly on the waters of the Strait of Georgia. More than once when a late afternoon wind whistled in, the *Texada Queen* came to our rescue and towed us back to Jedediah.

When we did make it to Pender Harbour, we often visited Jenny and Jimmy in the hospital cottages at Garden Bay. Jenny was much improved. Her asthma was under control. Jimmy was less content in this, his first experience away from his friends at Rouse Bay and Lasqueti. He had sold the *Quit* and was grounded. But his gregarious nature attracted almost everyone in the small community of Garden Bay, and the tiny hospital cottage was a gathering place for many of the pioneers and old-time fishermen of the coast.

When winter lifted her shroud, golden drifts of daffodils were revealed. Many seasons ago the homesteaders on Jedediah had planted fields of daffodils, whose blossoms were bright yellow and double in form, and now the bulbs had proliferated over the whole homestead. The boys and I enjoyed watching them open to their full glory. Many boatloads of visitors came each spring just to see the fields of daffodils.

The warmer weather also brought spring activities and interests. We soon shed our cabin fever, and boatloads of visitors arrived. The boys continued their correspondence schooling. It proved to be very successful academically, but socially it was a failure. They needed their friends and peers.

Ed did not return to the island to visit us. He wrote many letters, which the boys and I answered. I thought it was time the two of us came to some agreement concerning our separation. Later that fall, Roger and Evan and I returned to Ed and Seattle. The boys enrolled in school and were pleased to be among the friends they had left. But before long, Ed and I were unhappy living together. My sons and I moved to an apartment near their school. I found work in an accounting office and attended evening courses at the University of Washington. Ed and I tried reconciliation, to no avail. In the end we were divorced amicably. He kept the business and I was awarded my sons and Jedediah.

This was a sad and stressful period. Not only had I lost my marriage, I had also divorced Jedediah, temporarily. Again I relied on the Ryan family to care for the island, while I supported myself and the boys in the city.

During the time I attended evening classes at the university, I met Albert Palmer. He was enrolled in graduate school at the same time he was working for Fisheries Research Institute at the university. During the Second World War he had been a first mate on merchant marine ships in the Pacific. Our shared love of the outdoors and the sea brought us close together. We were married in 1959, when I was thirty-nine years of age and he was thirty-eight.

Our goal was to return to Jedediah. To accomplish this, we needed to salt away enough money to live there for a long time. We purchased a rundown nursery and landscaping business in Seattle—a venture that was aided by my position as garden editor of the *Seattle Post-Intelligencer*. By this time, Evan was in junior high school and Roger was attending a college near home.

Al decided to make one more trip to Alaska for the Fisheries Research Institute, then resign from the university and join me in running Palmer Gardens. While he was away, I made one more effort to find suitable caretakers for Jedediah, as the Ryan family were planning to move to Lasqueti. I placed an ad in the *Nanaimo Free Press* and received many interesting replies. One, from a family of twelve called Mann, interested me particularly. I answered it, arranging to meet them in Nanaimo. At that meeting we agreed to another get-together at their home on De Courcy Island. I was a bit apprehensive, as this island had been the headquarters in the 1930s of the infamous Brother Twelve and his notorious colony of believers, but we accepted their application and engaged them as caretakers.

I chartered a small tugboat from Nanaimo to haul the Manns, their belongings, my boys and myself to Jedediah. It was a distance of about twenty-five miles upcoast. Later in the summer, the Manns made several trips back to De Courcy to pick up lumber, furniture, home-canned fruit and vegetables—plus two milk cows.

The morning of the departure was quite frantic. Imagine stirring ten young ones out of bed at four in the morning, packing up their possessions, and loading the entire family into a tugboat to sail off to a place they had never seen before. Shirley, the mother, was almost nine months pregnant with her eleventh child. The little ones were fascinated by the adventure and the older ones were a bit more apprehensive. The four older boys, Danny, Ronnie, Alfie and Vernon, were engrossed in the workings of the

Earl (at left) and Shirley (at back) Mann, friends and caretakers of
Jedediah, with their eleven children, 1961.

tugboat, while the girls were busy taking care of the very little
ones. The babies, Carol and Norman, were bundled up in blan-
kets and placed in boxes for safety. Linda, the oldest child,
watched out for the ones who were running around the deck.
The middle girls Julie, Jennifer and Lennis were huddled together
in the galley when they were not helping with child care.

The summer day was calm with billowy clouds dancing
above. As we approached Jedediah, the young ones were becoming restless, and Julie and Jennifer had got very seasick. Lennis
and Linda tried to help them as best they could. We arrived at
Jedediah in the late afternoon. Dusk was creeping into Home
Bay. The tide was high and the skipper of the tugboat was able to
tie up at Jimmy's dock so that we could disembark. We trudged

up the hill to the house and tried to make everyone comfortable for the night. The skipper took off to anchor outside of the bay in deep water, until the tide was full the next morning.

At dawn, the tug returned to Jimmy's dock. The older boys, Linda and the adults had a quick cup of coffee and a biscuit before running down to unload the boat. Everyone pitched in while the tide was high and unloaded the Mann family's possessions onto the dock. Then we walked in a caravan, up and down from the dock to the house, carrying bags, boxes, baskets and bundles of gear this large family would need. Shirley stayed in the house, attempting to find spaces to put everything. She was amazing in her fortitude and endurance. But during one of my trips to the house, she said, "Mary, I'm getting pretty tired."

I took her hand and walked her to a chair. "Take care," I said, "or you'll have the baby too soon."

"It's too late," she moaned. "I feel like—" She didn't finish. Her water had broken.

Her husband Earl helped me get her to bed quickly. I had the older boys, along with Roger and Evan, put the little ones in the rowboat and go across the bay to play on Sandy Beach, so they would not hear their mother's distress. Then Earl went to find a large piece of plywood. This he placed over the mattress of the bed, covered by a flannel sheet. Then he disappeared.

Somehow I didn't panic. Something comes over you at a time of crisis to carry you through. I knew nothing about birthing—I had had two Caesarean births. Shirley had gone through this ten times before. She went in and out of consciousness, alternately giving me instructions through clenched teeth and screaming, "Get it out!"

I did my best to reassure her that all would be well, and I prayed. Then I thought of the thousands of pioneer women who had gone through childbirth alone. I had no type of pain killer in the house. If I had had a bottle of aspirin at that moment I would have taken half of it myself and given Shirley the other half! Instead, I got busy. I found some scissors and stout linen thread, put a kettle of water on the stove to boil, found a dishpan and some clean cloths. Every once in a while Earl appeared at the kitchen door, and once I asked him for the first aid kit. And did he have any notion where the drops for the baby's eyes might be? He fumbled about the stacks of supplies and found a small bottle with an eye dropper. Then he darted out the door.

Shirley's cries were loud and clear as she kept repeating, "Get it out!" I ran to her side, held her firmly and said, "Push! Push, Shirley!" She had such courage and such unyielding strength. Perspiration bathed her entire body; she gasped and heaved and bore down. Her hands clenched the sides of the plywood as she worked. "Push down, Shirley!" I kept shouting, while I held her hand ever so tight. With my other hand I wiped her forehead. She gave a piercing scream, and at that instant a miracle happened. A tiny head appeared, covered in a thin sac of mucus and blood. I put my hands on the baby's neck and supported the head, neck and shoulders. The new one slipped from Shirley's body, into my hands. Now what to do? Shirley slumped back on the bed and fell asleep.

I tied and cut the baby's cord. With the eye dropper, I applied the antiseptic solution to his eyes. Rubbing and cleaning his arms and legs with clean cloths, I noticed how tiny and blue his body was. I placed him in a pan of warm water then cold water, hoping this would stimulate his circulation. He came around and let out a few more screams. All was well. I cleaned Shirley's bed, changed the linen and washed her. She was exhausted. I laid the little one down next to her, and ran out on the front verandah, waving a towel and shouting, "It's a boy!" Soon the Mann brothers and sisters and Roger and Evan appeared on the scene. What joy to see their faces as they looked at the newest baby of the family. Now there were eleven.

Linda took the baby in her arms lovingly and cradled him. The other girls and the small boys took turns holding him, while the big boys just stood back and slouched off out the back door to do their own thing.

The next few days were busy ones for the Mann family as they unpacked and settled in. Shirley and the new one did well. She and Earl named him Wesley. He is the only white child known to have been born on Jedediah. Some aboriginal children were probably born there, as local Native groups spent time on Jedediah in summer to gather clams, berries and other foods.

Shirley Mann with her baby, Wesley, 1961. He made his appearance just a few hours after I helped move all the Manns and their belongings to Jedediah, and he is the only white child known to have been born on the island.

My sons and I stayed on with the Manns for a few more days, but it was late August and we had to get back. Evan and Roger had to return to school and I needed to get to work on our new nursery. Al was due back from Alaska around the same time.

The public telephone at Rouse Bay had been disconnected and the Phillips family had moved to Vancouver, so our only way of calling for transportation from the island was by radiotelephone aboard a tugboat. The boys, a few of the Mann youngsters and I hiked over to Deep Bay and found a tug anchored there. We hailed the crew and asked them to call a water taxi from Pender Harbour to come to Jedediah and pick us up the next day.

On our way back along the trail, we saw two raccoons scrounging around on the beach at Boom Bay, digging out clams for a feast. When they saw us they scurried away into the tall grass. One of them walked with a limp. Often raccoons lose their claws from trying to open the shells of clams and oysters. They also feed on crabs, other mollusks and stranded fish, and they are a real nuisance to fruit and vegetable gardeners.

The tide was high in the early morning. I awoke with the dawn and prepared my two boys for an early start. Shirley was up feeding the baby when we noticed the water taxi speeding into the bay. It was very difficult for us all to say goodbye. I felt especially melancholy about leaving the family alone on the island. They were a hardy bunch, originally from Alberta, but they were not accustomed to coastal life. In the early days they did not care for oysters, clams and other seafood. It was a good thing we had started a vegetable garden. The apple, pear, plum and other fruit trees later produced a bumper crop, and enough deer, sheep and goats grazed in the orchard to keep the family fed.

The water taxi sped us into Pender Harbour. From there we took a bus to Vancouver and then another to Seattle. Roger and Evan returned to school. I continued to write for the *Post-Intelligencer* paper and looked forward to Al's return.

A letter from Jenny was awaiting me in Seattle. We had stopped in to see her and Jimmy on our way home, and I had told them of my divorce and remarriage. Jenny had improved and they were now living in a hospital cottage near St. Mary's. The boys had been especially pleased to see Jimmy. Jenny's letter read:

Please forgive me for not writing you long before this, the old eyes have given me a lot of trouble in spite of the treatments. We are very sorry to hear in your letter the circumstances which have made you so unhappy and sorry old Jedediah should be a part of the cause. I know how hard you both had to work, after the heavy losses due to the failure of the business. Long work hours are apt to over-tax the nerves. I believe you have done the right thing and sincerely hope that any resentment will pass away with time.

I do hope that when you come to Jedediah this summer you will come to us and talk. We shall not question you, just tell us enough to ease your mind and heart. We will try to help and comfort you with sympathetic understanding. Please come to us as you would your own parents.

How are your two boys? They are truly fine fellows and sincerely hope they are well and happy. Easter will soon be with us, a time of promise and renewal of life. May it be a glorious Easter for you all. Jimmy is in bed with a heavy cold, he has acute bronchitis, so I have insisted that he stay down in bed. He won't get out of the door as I have hidden all his pants. It's the only way to handle a stubborn Scotchman! We shall be looking forward to seeing you this summer, also the boys.

Thank you for your letter, and forgive me for neglecting to answer you sooner. I hope to hear from you anytime you wish to drop a line.

Now I must say good night and God bless you. Chin up, my dear. Jimmy joins in with love and kindest thoughts of you.

Al and I spent the following weeks and months working hard on the small, rundown nursery and making it productive and profitable. Evan was enrolled in college and worked with us in the nursery on weekends and school holidays. Roger changed his mind about college and joined the United States Army instead. He served in Germany for three years before coming home again. When he got back he joined us, working in the nursery as a landscaper. With him he brought back from Germany a baby girl he had fathered there. Her name was Carolin, and she was a sweet and loving child. A year or two after returning home, Roger married a girl from Seattle, Rachel. She was an honours graduate of the University of Washington who had trained as a physical therapist. They had two more children: Sally, then a year and a half later Andy arrived. We enjoyed our three wonderful grandchildren.

Meanwhile, the Mann family remained on Jedediah and sent many interesting letters describing their life there. One of Shirley's letters gave us an indication of the amount of food and other supplies a family of eleven needed for one winter.

The Mann and Ryan families enjoy a beach picnic, 1961.

Some of the Mann children examine a beached sea lion up close, 1964.
Left to right: Lennis, Linda, Jennifer, Norman, Julie and Vernon.

It was fairly nice this week, no rain, wind or storms. We
brought over to the island twenty-nine sacks of potatoes, three hundred pounds of turnips, two hundred
pounds of carrots and several boxes of pumpkin, squash
and cabbage, six hundred pounds of flour, two hundred
pounds of dried beans, one hundred pounds of rice, a
forty-five-gallon barrel of molasses, one hundred
pounds of salt, one hundred pounds of peas, two cases
of margarine, one case of lard, one case toilet tissue,
soap and I guess that's about all. Our vegetable garden
didn't produce too well this summer, we just ate it all as
it ripened. We canned over seven hundred quarts of
fruit from the trees.

The cows are milking good with so much pasture to
roam. We are cutting a fine crop of hay with the scythe,

it appears to be of good quality. The cows will need it this winter.

Danny and Vernon and I went over to Lasqueti to visit the Ryan family. We brought them some milk and butter I had made, along with cookies and jars of fruit. We had a great time together.

Earl, Alfie and Danny just got back from De Courcy. They got all finished up there, except for some lumber. They have brought to Jedediah 6 loads of supplies.

During the last load, the boat engine blew a gasket so they got as far as Ballenas Island. They stayed there for the night to repair the engine. Started out in the early morning, but a wind came up. So they stayed another day. The next day they ventured out and it was really blowing. They noticed a tug in the bay and asked the crew what the weather report was. They said that the wind was ceasing, according to the report. The tug was going to start out for Lasqueti with a boom of logs and the captain told Earl they could come along with the boom. They were pretty lucky to get a lift with the tug to Lasqueti, then home to Jedediah.

We are content and happy here, and the new baby Wesley is a healthy, lively one and all the others are well too. We send our love, write to us soon.

Al and I stayed with the nursery business for ten years. Each summer we hoped to visit Jedediah, and finally, almost the last year we kept the business, we were able to make the trip. Al bought a small dory-type boat with two 50-horsepower outboard engines. The boat was eighteen feet long and quite beamy.

During late summer, we cruised from Seattle to Jedediah. We followed a part of the route taken by Francisco Eliza and José Maria Narvaez in 1791. First we travelled through the

American San Juan Islands, then crossed the 49th parallel into Canadian waters. We sailed to East Point on Saturna Island. This island was named after the Spanish naval schooner *Saturna*, which Narvaez commanded. Modern-day schooners and sailors flock to the island during the Saturna Island lamb barbecue, each July 1.

On Jedediah, we enjoyed visiting with the Mann family and had time to survey what should be done to ready the house for us. Our hope was to retire to Jedediah as soon as possible.

Al cut shakes from cedar blocks with a froe to replace the roof of the house and work shed. The older Mann boys helped him find cedar blocks that had washed up on the beach. They were already busy collecting drifting logs that had escaped from floating log booms. They rowed out and attached lines to the loose logs, towed them into Home Bay and tied them securely. Every few weeks a log salvage buyer would come by and buy the logs. Eventually the boys applied for a log salvage licence of their own and did well.

Shirley and I had many talks about her children. She believed it was time for them to move to Lasqueti, as their father was cruel and cunning, and life with him was becoming unbearable. Also, they wanted to attend school with other children. I agreed with her.

We stayed for about ten days before going back to Seattle in our

Norman, Wesley and Carol Mann going to Sandy Beach, 1965.

boat. We knew it was time for us to retire permanently to Jedediah. We listed our home and business with a real estate firm, and while we waited for buyers, we searched for and purchased the necessary tools, equipment and supplies we would need for living on the island.

First our home sold, then the business. Finally, in 1971, we were ready for Jedediah. We applied for and were granted Canadian Landed Immigrant status. A few years later we became Canadian citizens.

The house at Home Bay, 1971. That year my second husband Al Palmer and I moved to the island permanently.

Our main household goods were loaded on trucks in Seattle, taken to a dock at Vancouver, then carried to Jedediah by tug and barge. We made many trips from Seattle to the Sunshine Coast. We kept an old Ford pickup truck at Buccaneer Bay, near Sechelt, to drive to and from Seattle to bring back more tools and equipment. After a few months, we made a trip to the mainland in search of farm equipment and farm animals. We had to load a hay bailer, tractor, binder, seeder and other huge pieces of farming equipment aboard the barge. We also loaded Suffolk sheep, white-faced cattle, a Jersey milk cow and some poultry onto the barge, and freighted everything to Jedediah.

Now what to do with this equipment and livestock? We were gardeners, but had never had a chance to learn how to take care of animals and operate farm machinery. We hired a farmer from Lasqueti to show us the ropes, and also sent for agricultural publications and bulletins from colleges and universities.

The most useful book we had—a loose-leaf binder of mimeographed pages called "Old-Fashioned Recipe Book," written by Carla Emery of Kendrick, Idaho—was a gift to us. It was as thick as the old Sears catalogue, bursting with useful ideas on animal husbandry, home industries, recipes for food and ways to preserve it by canning, drying, pickling and winter storage, and home health remedies. The many chapters on the care of sheep became our bible. Shearing, carding and weaving wool were included in the book. We tried the author's recipes for ale, wine, ginger and root beer. Often our experiments would blow up in the basement, but we loved trying. When visitors appeared we gave them samples of our homemade refreshments. Sometimes this made us friends for life, sometimes quite the opposite. We owe much to Carla for her fine book of instructions. City folks like us would have failed in many ways without her guidance. We still had many failures during our farming years, but we weathered them all and kept on enjoying both the successes and failures.

In Carla's book there is a poem called "Mama's Day," in which she describes a day when she milked the cows, fed them hay, did a washing, mopped the floors, cooked home-dried fruit, swept the parlour, made the beds, baked a dozen loaves of bread, split some wood, cleaned the lamps, churned the butter, baked a cake, gathered some eggs and chased the calves back into the pen, went out and chased them in again, returned to the house and set the table, cooked the supper, washed the dishes, fed the cat, sprinkled the clothes, mended a basket full of clothes, then opened the old organ and began to play "When You Come to the End of a Perfect Day." Life on Jedediah in

A homesteader at Home Bay, 1906.

1972 was not much different than the life of the Mama of the poem written in the early 1900s.

During our first summer of retirement on Jedediah, both Jenny and Jimmy passed away. We were notified that their ashes would be scattered in Home Bay. On the appointed day, we rowed our boat out to meet Canon Alan Greene's ship, the *John Antle*. Canon Greene arrived wearing his black and white vestments. Solemnly, he stood alone in the prow of the forty-six-foot vessel and performed the burial service. "For inasmuch as it has pleased the almighty God in his mercy to take the souls of our dear friends Jenny and Jimmy Riddell," he intoned to sea and sky, "we therefore commit their ashes to the deep."

After the service we invited Canon Greene into our home. He changed his vestments. We helped him anchor his vessel in deep water outside the bay. He stepped into our small rowboat and we rowed into Jimmy's dock. "I remember when I performed

Jenny and Jimmy's marriage ceremony right on this spot," he said. "We will all miss them. It was a strange relationship, a sweet, gentle woman and a rough-and-ready fisherman, yet they had a wonderful life together."

On our short walk from the dock to the house, Canon Greene commented that he had ministered to a flock of more than two thousand five hundred people, strewn some two hundred and fifty miles between Halfmoon Bay and Cape Scott. In some cases he had christened three generations of one family.

When we got to the house, Al showed Canon Greene into the parlour to a chair with a view of the sea, and I brought in a tray of hot tea and some fruit and cakes. Canon Greene told us he was from Ontario, but had lived on the coast for nearly fifty years. His father, Canon Dicky Greene of Orillia, Ontario, was a clergyman who was immortalized by Stephen Leacock as Canon Drone in *Sunshine Sketches of a Little Town*.

"While my brother and I were lads," Canon Greene told us, "we were forever on boats on Lake Ontario. During my student years at Wycliffe College in Toronto, I worked as a deckhand and purser on the Great Lakes. In 1911 I moved to Vananda, on Texada Island, to command the little vessel *Eirene*." As I filled his teacup, he told us, "You know, this is my last official duty. I have retired now, after forty years of ministry on the coast."

"We hope you will stop by to visit us often in your retirement," Al said. Greene answered, "The Lord willing."

The day was slipping away, and Canon Greene stood up from his chair. "It's best I leave you now," he said. "The trip back to Pender Harbour will take the *John Antle* a couple of hours. I hesitate to travel now during the darkness of night."

Al and I rowed him out to his vessel and bade him farewell. After the *John Antle* left, Al and I took a few moments to say our final farewells to Jenny and Jimmy. A slight summer breeze ruffled the surface of the water. Lightly a gossamer veil seemed to

Our grandson Andy with new lambs, spring 1980.

surround us, as darkness fell. We were not alone on Jedediah. Jenny's and Jimmy's spirits would be with us always.

Early spring is the usual lambing time, but a few ewes straggle along later. On our way out to the fields one morning, we noticed one of the late ones. She seemed to be struggling. Al quickly ran over to her and yelled, "She's giving birth, and it looks like trouble." He rolled up his sleeves and thrust his hand and arm deep inside the ewe. Carefully he turned the tiny lamb about so it would be born with its tiny feet first. Blood and mucus covered the new arrival. It stood up on its four legs weakly. The old ewe cleaned her newborn. Al directed its nose up to the mother's milk bag and the lamb sucked with vigour. This first milk, the colostrum, contains nutrients and antibiotics needed for the animal's survival. Soon the new lamb was bouncing about full of life. The ewe seemed proud, and each time the lamb took a bit of milk, its tiny tail wiggled in delight.

We were glad to see the ewe care for her newborn so well.

Occasionally a ewe will abandon her offspring at birth, and then the first priority is to get another nursing ewe to accept the orphan. This can take all the shepherd's ingenuity. The ewe is held in a small pen so that the lamb can get close to its "foster mother." The new lamb is then encouraged to suckle the ewe. If this fails, the shepherd milks out the stubborn birth mother's colostrum and places it in a sterile bottle with a lamb nipple on the end. The milk is warmed and the new lamb is kept warm and dry while taking milk from the bottle.

Our lambing barn on the island had no power for heat lamps. To keep an orphan lamb warm and alive, we filled a ten-gallon crock with hot water so the young ones could lean on it for warmth. The crock needed refilling every twelve hours. During cold spring weather we would often bring the orphans indoors to keep warm in a small pen in the kitchen.

While we were working with the old ewe and newborn, we looked up and were startled to see three young people watching us. They introduced themselves as Ann, Tom and Brian. "We are from the Coastal Mission of Chemainus," Tom said. "We hope you don't mind us invading your privacy."

"Not in the least," Al replied. "You are most welcome."

I blurted out, "We usually boil missionaries in oil, but you seem a bit thin for a feast." Ann looked carefully at me then began to laugh. We all looked down at the new lamb, and decided mother and young were doing well without us.

Tom asked us if they could be of help around the farm. "We are experts at cutting wood, roofing, or any other needs you may have."

Al thanked them graciously but said we were doing well on our own.

I noticed Ann had a lovely wicker picnic basket in her hand, and I invited them to stay for lunch. Brian said they would love to stay and tell us about their mission.

When we reached the kitchen, I started a fire in the stove. Soon the tea water was boiling. Ann opened her basket and put out a variety of lovely sandwiches. I added tea and dessert. We shared a fine meal.

"We cover an area from Chemainus to Alaska," Tom began, "spreading the gospel and sharing the lives of people in the coastal villages we visit."

"Are you always welcome?" I asked.

"No, not always. If the people do not wish to know about the Lord, we do not push them on the subject. We just become friends, and try in time to help them understand our mission."

Al said, "We are not of any particular religious faith, yet we do believe in a superior being or force of some sort. Just being on a farm with animals, on an isolated island, you quickly understand there is a power stronger than you watching over all."

The afternoon passed swiftly and we walked back to Deep Bay with Ann, Tom and Brian.

On our way to Deep Bay, we watched a flock of goats grazing in the meadow. They shied away when they noticed us, although they were becoming a bit more tame now that we lived permanently on the island. Tom was amazed at their appearance. He asked what kind of goats they were.

Al answered, "We are not certain. The old-timers tell us that when the Spanish explorers travelled along the Pacific Coast from Mexico to Alaska, they dropped off milking goats along the way, to graze on the islands and to be picked up later on their return trip. They used these goats for fresh milk and meat aboard the ships."

"Look how beautiful their coats are, so shiny and sleek," Anne commented.

"What a capital idea," Tom chimed in. "We should do the same aboard our little ship."

"No way," was Anne and Brian's reply.

In spring the trees in the orchard burst into bloom, and the lambs and calves were born. I watched many a mother clean and warm her newborn on Jedediah.

Brian reached down and touched a blue flower like a hyacinth. He remarked, "You have so many camas here. Did you know that the Indians of this region really appreciated the true camas? They called it 'quamash.' It was their most important food. There is more romance and adventure clustered about the camas root and flower than almost any other native plant."

He reached down and picked one of the dark blue flowers and, examining it carefully, told us that the early Pacific explorers recorded that the roots saved them from starvation. Camas fields were tribal property, jealously guarded against the trespass of rival clans. Wars were sometimes caused by disputes over questions of possession or boundary. The Natives had a difficult time understanding why the white man was privileged to usurp these possessions, and destroy the camas meadows with a plough.

"Once a Nez Perce woman told me how you cook the

roots," Brian continued. "First you make a large hole in the ground, line it with flat stones, and build a fire upon the stones. When they are red hot, rake out the coals and cover the hot stones with wild grass. Then upon the grass place the camas, and over this place another layer of grass. Then cover all, first with mats of wet cedar and then dirt, and over all build a fire which is kept burning for two nights and a day. The pit should not be opened or poked into during this time, or the camas will be spoiled. Indian medicine practitioners pounded the bulbs in a mortar and used the material as a poultice to cure boils, rheumatism, bruises and sprains, and to relieve pain in general. Also some unscrupulous medicine men mixed the root with a little tobacco, to give a person severe nausea, in order to secure a heavy fee for making them well again, after they recovered from the mixture."

We reached the site of their mission ship in Deep Bay. Tom untied the dinghy at the water's edge and jumped into the boat. Brian and Anne stepped aboard and Tom rowed them out to the vessel. Al and I wished them well on their mission up north. Al yelled out to their boat to return on their way back south for a visit with us.

Many times in our years on Jedediah they returned to us with good cheer and a willingness to help out with our farm chores, and they gave us accounts of their missions to people of the coast. In a way their dedication was a continuation of Canon Alan Greene's work after his retirement.

That first settled summer on the island was glorious for Al and me. We had shaken off the anxieties and pressure of the city. Each day on Jedediah brought to us new challenges, but the urgent tasks could often wait long enough for us to stop and evaluate the many facets of our new way of life.

That summer and for some time after, I still wrote regularly for the *Seattle Times*, and we installed a radiotelephone to keep

Our grandchildren Andy, Carolin and Sally in the orchard with a
young calf and our dogs Pepper (left) and Belle.

in touch with my editor there. Every ten days or two weeks I
would travel from Jedediah to Seattle. The contact with the
paper was a safety net, in case we found living on Jedediah
tedious and unrewarding. This never happened. Each day on
Jedediah was a treasure. I became so engrossed in the island that
eventually I relinquished my newspaper work, and wrote only
for a few journals of interest.

During the autumn of our first year, we had the brief pleasure of the company of a homing pigeon. The bird seemed quite
comfortable with us. One morning it landed outside by the
kitchen door and hopped in toward the cooking stove. Al
picked it up and examined it, and found a ring band on one leg.
He made a note of the band numbers and wrote a letter to the
Ministry of Environment in Victoria.

A few weeks later we received a reply from the Ministry.
"Thank you for your recent note about the banded Rock Dove,"

it read. "As Rock Doves are domestic birds, many owners mark their birds with private bands. We do not keep records of dove banding. However, I can tell from the band number the bird was born in 1970 and was registered with the Racing Pigeon Association that begins with the letter P."

The racing pigeon rested at our home only for a few days, then flew away—toward its home, we hope.

On the same day the pigeon arrived, a power-ful log salvage tug bear-ing the name *Vulture* steamed full-power into Home Bay. The thirty-six-foot tug swirled about the bay in search of stray beached or float-ing logs that had escaped broken booms. Salvage tugs usually have con-tracts with towing com-panies to round up any logs that escape their booms.

Al makes the mail run to Lasqueti Island. Often we went over together, and the trip became an occasion to stop and visit friends.

A log salvage boat must often do its work during tremen-dous storms, so the crews often lead exhilarating and dangerous lives. A log "jerker" must sometimes jump from log to log in storms, securing them back inside the boom. He must also be capable of jerking logs off the beach. It is not unusual for a cable to break under the strain and for the metal "dog" or pin, attached to the stubborn log, to pull loose and fly back toward the boat with a mighty force. Many a mark from a detached "dog" is imprinted on salvage boats.

Aft of the wheelhouse of the tug in our bay stood a burly, round man shouting orders to shore. The person taking the orders was a diminutive and nimble lady hopping lightly over beached logs. She was fastening a cable with a dog attached to each log, as an unending rumble of expletives resounded from the tug. Capably and swiftly she accomplished her task. Each log jerked and rolled over the beach, and quickly was floating in the water behind the tug. They continued working the logs free of the beach while we watched in astonishment at their swiftness and skill. When they had removed several lost logs from the beach, Al motioned for them to come ashore. They tied their prize logs together securely behind the tug, towed their catch out to deeper water and threw out an anchor. A sturdy rowboat was tossed over the side and the two of them rowed to our beach. The man put out his large hand and announced he was Sam Lamont and his deckhand was Anne Clemence.

As they disembarked, Sam tied a sturdy line from the rowboat to a heavy wire cable we had embedded in concrete in a huge beach rock. Anne was holding a large wicker basket filled with goodies. I reached out and helped her up the rocks to the pathway. She was a small, pert, dainty lady, most capable without my helpful hand. But I extended it as a gesture of friendship.

Anne said she was originally from Seven Oaks, in England. She had been trained as a nurse and had been on duty at the hospital at Pender Harbour when she met Sam. During this time, the late 1960s, killer whales were being caught and held for study in pens at Pender Harbour. Sam was part of the project, and Anne became fascinated with the whales and Sam, and also Sam with Anne.

"How are you folks enjoying the coast?" Sam asked, his thick black eyebrows raised quizzically.

Out trekking Jedediah with friends, 1982. Left to right: Sam Lamont, me and Anne Clemence. Sam and Anne are legendary figures in the Pender Harbour area. Sam always wore his suspenders, but seldom wore a shirt.

"We believe we are in heaven," Al answered.

Sam pulled tightly on his thick red suspenders and gave them a snap. He was shirtless. (Sam rarely wore a shirt, as we learned later.) He continued, "How come a couple of Yankees settled here?"

"Hey Sam, we love it here, just like you," I blurted out. He threw back his head and gave out a laugh that shook his huge body.

As Anne made her way up the rocks and to the path, I noticed how immaculately she was dressed. Incredible! She appeared ready for tea at the Empress Hotel after her hard morning as deckhand on a log salvage tug. Anne was also an accomplished gourmet cook and seamstress, and knew how to show patience with a robust fellow like Sam. She understood that for all of Sam's blustering and bellowing, he was the finest, kindest and most compassionate of fellows. On most occasions, she was in control.

Sam had brought along a fine fish. "Give me a sharp knife," he said, "and I'll cut this fellow up for our dinner." I obliged. Al, Anne and I ran down to the garden to dig a few new potatoes and pull some carrots and beets from the soil. We had a feast. Anne's fine butter tarts and tea finished off the meal. As we ate, they entertained us with accounts of their life aboard the *Vulture*. They also told us they were building a cottage near the water at

Sam Lamont and Anne Clemence's salvage tug the *Vulture*.

Pender Harbour, and the *Vulture* was tied up at a dock in front of their cottage, ready for action day or night. These two people were unique. We were grateful and honoured to have them as coastal friends.

As dusk enfolded the sky, Sam remarked, "Well, Anne, we'd best pull anchor and leave." Anne rose from the table and began to clear the dishes. We had not yet installed a sink, so the dishes went into a pan of hot water on the back of the stove to be washed, then in another large pan to be rinsed. Anne and I finished the cleanup. Al filled her wicker basket with vegetables from the garden, and we gave them a gallon of milk and cream from Rosie, our good Jersey cow.

Walking down the path to the beach, Anne bent over to admire the coral bells in bloom. "Mary, my plants aren't in bloom yet," she remarked. "You have it a bit warmer here on Jedediah than we have in the Harbour." I picked a few blossoms and placed them in her small hands.

We were sorry to see them leave. But the *Vulture* found its way to Jedediah on many occasions over the years. When we heard the roar of the mighty engines nearing Jedediah, our spirits soared. Not only were Sam and Anne wonderful companions, they brought us many necessary items to make our lives more pleasant. One spring day they arrived with a complete bathroom set—a flushing toilet, bathtub and sink. Imagine our delight! Sam stayed to help Al pack the items up the path and later install the wonderful new fixtures. When we added a new kitchen onto the old house, Sam freighted over some large double windows for it.

Many times during the summer, Anne and Sam brought guests from along the coast and relatives of Anne's from England. One of our most interesting and inspiring visitors was Edith Iglauer Daly, author of many books including the bestselling *Fishing with John*, on her life as a fisherman's wife and partner on the coast of BC. We were completely fascinated by Edith, her husband John and her two sons. Edith was most supportive, and she urged me on to write my book on Jedediah.

A day or two after Anne and Sam's first visit, Al and I were walking along on the beach when we noticed a glass bottle snuggled in a nest of seaweed. Al reached down and picked up the bottle, and struggled to unfasten the cork which was securely sealed with paraffin. Inside the bottle was a piece of paper which read:

To whom it may concern:
The bottle which you found was sent as an experiment by members of Cloverley Elementary School in North Vancouver. We are interested in the travel of the bottle and its final destination. The bottle originated in Burrard Inlet at Vancouver, British Columbia. If you would be so kind as to reply to us concerning your find. Please enclose in your letter the following information: Where the bottle was found (the closest city or town), date when the bottle was found. Please offer a brief explanation of the circumstances surrounding the find of our bottle. Please include your name and address for further correspondence. Your co-operation in our experiment will be deeply appreciated.

It was signed by a teacher and the address was included. Promptly the next morning I answered the letter, but to our disappointment, we did not hear from the students or the teachers at the school.

At dawn one morning not long after, as we looked up at the sky, we saw a mature eagle laboriously flapping its broad wings, a newborn lamb clutched in its huge talons. This happens in the wild. When the mother sheep is busy giving birth to the second or third lamb, she cannot fend off the attack of an eagle or raven. Most of the birthing sheep stay inside the barn for protection, but sometimes they birth outdoors. We were helpless, and sickened by the sight, but this is a part of the nature of things. For some time we had been considering getting a trained sheepdog, and this event made up our minds.

At high tide a few days later, Al and I crossed the Strait of

Georgia to French Creek, where we kept the old pickup truck. We drove to Vancouver and went from kennel to kennel to find the right dog. But it was to no avail—we could not find a border collie. At one of the kennels where we stopped to inquire, they had no collies but they bred registered Samoyeds. We were invited to look at their new puppies. Unfortunately, once you see a Samoyed puppy, your heart is lost forever. We cuddled up to a little female fluffy Samoyed puppy who went home in our arms. We named her Belle. She was useless as a sheepdog, but she was a prize at keeping varmints away from the chicken house and geese pens. No weasel, mink or raccoon could get near the poultry, day or night. Belle was a beautiful, loving and very useful animal. We enjoyed her companionship for many years on Jedediah.

Harvest time, 1972. Al and me with our beloved dogs Belle (left) and Pepper.

Belle was our only dog for a year, then we bought a trained border collie named Pepper from the fellow we had bought our Suffolk sheep from. She had a black and white face, like salt and pepper. Belle was pleased to have a soulmate. Each dog had her chores and knew them well.

Years later, after old age had claimed both Belle and Pepper, we searched for another trained border collie. Our granddaughter

Carolin found a fine dog for us in Courtenay, BC, from a dog trainer named John Wickson. "Fly," our new border collie, was the most intelligent, well-trained animal we ever had. She was as fast as a southeast wind during a storm. Her training was unbelievable, and so was her loyalty and devotion. We still enjoy the companionship of Fly. She is old now, but like us, she has earned her retirement.

Chapter

4

DURING OUR EARLY YEARS ON JEDEDIAH, AL AND I were often visited by a young neighbour, James Dougan. He was the nephew of our good friend, Bill Cox. These were the Coxes and Dougans who operated the logging company at Anderson Bay, on the southern tip of Texada Island.

Jim had grown up at Anderson Bay and after logging was finished in the early 1960s, he moved with his family to Cobble Hill, BC. When he was in his early twenties, Jim returned to Texada and lived near his uncle Bill. He built a fine log cabin, kept a few milk goats and made his living by picking salal and huckleberry branches and selling them to florists. His life was interesting and fulfilling, but he needed a companion to share his adventures and challenges. We suggested he advertise in farm papers for a girl who would want to share his way of life. He advertised in British Columbia and Alberta, received several responses and chose one from Alberta.

Jim met Margaret and she soon moved to Texada with him. Three girls and two boys arrived to expand the family to seven.

Around the same time, Jim Dougan's uncle Bill Cox decided he needed a companion too. With both Jim and Bill married, there was a veritable population boom on the south end of

Bill Cox, our neighbour from Texada Island, 1982. For many years, his family and the Dougan family ran a successful logging show on the south end of the island—a world apart from the more developed and populated north end.

Texada. In the 1960s, 1970s and 1980s, nine people inhabited the area.

Bill Cox, a confirmed bachelor after having been married twice, had bought two hundred acres on southern Texada and had retired there alone. He was very pleased with his way of doing things, but he too needed a soulmate.

Bill had a pen pal in Vancouver, who was a neighbour of a single golden-ager named Margaret Boyer. The friend wrote glowing reports of the virtues of Margaret, and Bill made the trip to Vancouver to check this lady out. They met and Cupid's arrow made a direct hit on both of them. The second new Margaret soon moved to Fulton Bay, on Texada. She found life on an isolated island to be a great change from living in Vancouver, but she adjusted quickly to Bill's life.

After Margaret arrived, she and Bill hosted an annual late-August barbecue for all their family and friends. People came by water and by air, and over the old logging road from Blubber Bay on the north end of Texada. The road trip was an experience only for the rough-and-ready ex-logging truck drivers—who tackled with ease steep grades such as the one known as

Break Your Ass Hill—and for the younger fellows, who came by motorcycle. Large sections of road were washed out and had to be temporarily repaired before the vehicle could go on. On these hot, dry August days, great billowing clouds of dust would have to be endured.

Guests who flew in on the air strip, which was built in 1951, were almost as brave. A few others arrived by float plane on the beach, and one year a helicopter set down on an open space in Bill's meadow, and the occupants jumped out and joined the party.

We always went by boat, with homemade apple pies and garden flowers for the tables. As we beached our boat, I would toss a few blossoms over the surface of the sea, to give the scene a festive air. "Old Original" whisky and other spirits were taken. Plenty of soda pop and juice was available to the young ones.

By midday the outdoor wooden tables were laden with goodies, including quantities of Bill's home-grown vegetables, store-bought sundries, fruits, homemade sausages and preserves. The meals ended with pies, cakes, cookies and ice cream. Entertainment was provided by Jim Dougan, who composed suitable songs for the occasion and sang them well while accompanying himself on his guitar. There were some old songs, too. Everyone gathered around in a loose circle, sitting on the grass to enjoy "Honky Tonk Man," "The Pub With No Beer," "Cold Cold Heart" and "The Tennessee Waltz." Little ones danced inside the circle while others clapped and joined in the singing.

One song that Al and I always requested began: "A little up north where the eagles soar, far away from the city smog, I built a shack in a rocky cove from the driftwood board and log. My soul was tired and my heart was down, so I left it all and asked old God to teach me peace of mind."

Around the tables, the old loggers exchanged tall tales of days when they had first logged the Texada area, settled in, and built cabins, cook houses and bunkhouses for the crew. A fine schoolhouse was built for the young ones. Stories of the school-marm were recounted with laughter.

The barbecue lasted for an entire weekend. Guests slept in their campers, tents, barns or wherever they could find a comfy spot for the night.

Roger and his wife Rachel, with Serena Ryan, 1980s.

Our whole family attended Bill's barbecue. Evan, Roger and his wife Rachel, their children Carolin, Sally and Andy came along, and if we had guests at the time of the bash, they came too.

One August day after Bill Cox's bash, we were all back on Jedediah sleeping in when we heard the roar of a helicopter overhead. Al was first up. He rushed out to see what was going on and found the cows scattering about the field as a helicopter attempted to land in the meadow.

Two young pilots emerged from the helicopter and shouted at Al. "Do you mind if we land here and wait a while for the fog to lift?"

"Where are you headed for?" Al called back.

"We work for the Highways Department of Greater Vancouver," one fellow answered. "We make a trip to the top of Texada about every third month to refill the propane tanks. They keep the beacon in operation, for signals to radio beams."

"You are certainly welcome to stay about," Al said, "but please turn off your propellers, as they frighten the cows from their pasture."

One of the pilots stopped the engine and the rotary blades. He asked, "Is there anything you would like us to move with our machine while we are here?"

"Well, now, you could move the old house for a better view of the horizon," I suggested.

Al suggested they move a large fibreglass tank we had found floating in our bay after a storm. If it could be moved to the top of the hill by the barn, water would flow down to the house by gravity. Our pump at the spring would pump water up to the tank.

The two men quickly manoeuvred the water tank by helicopter to the top of a small hill. Al and Roger guided the tank to its final resting place and laid planks under the tank to keep it level and secure.

Watching from below were Cal, Bruce and Gordon Jones. "We thought we'd better get over here and see what was happening with the helicopter," said Cal. "We were worried of an accident."

"No, Cal," Al said, "all is well, we are just moving the unmovable. But thanks for checking in on us."

Our good friends, the Jones family, were always available when we needed a helping hand. They had moved from Seattle about the same time Al and I retired to Jedediah. With the help of the two parents, Cal and Laurienni, the young sons established a thriving aquaculture business at Skerry Bay, Lasqueti

Island. Our families were very close and we spent many great times together over the years.

The fog was still thick on top of Texada, so I invited everyone in for coffee and cookies. As we enjoyed our treats we got to talking, and the pilots wanted to know why we were living on an isolated island all alone.

Al took the challenge. "Wouldn't you like living in paradise?" he replied.

This stopped the two fellows for a minute. Then they responded with a flow of questions. How do you get your groceries? Gas? Go to the doctor? Who are your neighbours? And on and on.

Gordon answered for us. "They grow most of their groceries, gas comes by barge, tug or fish boats and they don't need doctors with the healthy way they live, and neighbours and tourists by the hundreds drop by Mary and Al's, along with stopping by our place at Skerry Bay."

"Well, I guess you island folks got it pretty good," said the younger man, "but give me the city anytime." By this time the fog had lifted and they decided to be on their way. We thanked the two fellows again for helping us place the tank on the hill. Al ran down into the garden and brought back a sack full of garden

Evan enjoying a quiet moment with our border collie Pepper, 1980.

vegetables for the pilots to take back to the city.

The helicopter roared upward and over to Texada. Cal, Bruce and Gordon went down to the garden with Al to gather a few carrots, beets and salad greens to take back to Skerry Bay for Mrs. Jones to prepare for them.

After everyone had left, we began to plan how to connect the water from the spring to the new water tank on the hill, a distance of about a thousand feet. Roger suggested we might need a stronger gas pump at the spring to force the water uphill to the tank, and Al had plenty of two-inch plastic pipe and fittings to cover the area. All pros and cons were discussed until it was time to turn in for the night.

Before dawn the next morning, our closest neighbour on Bull Island, Rosalind Hildred, was pounding on our kitchen door. "Come and help us," she yelled. "My brother's boat is high and dry on the rocks."

Al was first up and Roger followed. They raced down to the beach, launched the rowboat with Rosalind and rowed over to

Roger and Rachel's home, finished at last, 1988. They lived there in the summer only, as their youngsters were in school.

our anchored-out twenty-two-foot boat. With full steam ahead they left the bay.

After an hour or two, Al and Roger returned to report that Rosalind's brother's boat was safe and free from the rocks. "Our boat didn't have enough power to pull the *Anne V. Fagan* from the reef," Al reported, "and the tide was starting to go out, so we hailed a large fish boat that was near the scene and it was pulled off safely."

The next week we received a note of thanks from Rosalind. "Bruce wishes to convey his thanks for your concern and assistance," she wrote. "He left for Vancouver right away, hopefully to get a fishing contract and some insurance. After retrieving his anchor and getting a rope out of his propeller whee what a day. Thanks for your help."

Rosalind was a flower child from Salt Spring Island, whose parents had allowed her to be a free spirit. In summer, she would jump aboard her brother's fish boat for some great adventures. As she grew older, her horizons widened. She trekked across Canada and wound up in New Jersey, married to a young black teacher. His parents did not approve of the marriage to a blonde Viking girl from the west coast, and Rosalind knew her family would also disapprove. Two sons were born, Aaron and Todd. When they were still quite young, Rosalind became disappointed in the marriage and the lifestyle. With her two tiny fellows, she made her way back to the west coast, where attitudes had not kept up with her and the two youngsters were not well accepted. So she bundled up her boys and travelled upcoast on one of her brother's fish boats to stay with an old school chum from Salt Spring Island. She heard he had moved up north to a small island near Lasqueti.

Bill, her old friend, was overjoyed to see her. His life had become extremely desolate and lonely. Rosalind, Aaron and Todd moved into Bill's dilapidated shack with him. Rosalind joined Bill in his plan to build a large wooden sailboat from salvaged logs and lumber, and they worked on the boat and lived on Bull Island for ten years.

Life was often difficult for them all. Living an isolated life on a small island is a challenge at the best of times, and Bill was his own person and very moody and self-centred. For food they fished and hunted deer and wild sheep. Rosalind kept a great garden and worked long hours keeping body and soul together for them

Aaron and Todd, sons of Rosalind Hildred, our friend on Bull Island, 1981.

all. Bill meditated. Rosalind and her sons had many great times, also many extremely unbearable experiences.

Al and I always welcomed Bill, Rosalind and the young ones to Jedediah. We also stopped by Bull Island on our way to Lasqueti. Al was especially interested in the progress of the fine boat they were building. Bill was very resourceful in his use of tools and made many ingenious woodworking tools from bits and pieces.

Later that fall, on a beautiful, crisp morning, Al burst through the kitchen door with a bushel of ripe red tomatoes from the garden. "We'd better get busy and start to put these in jars," he announced. I stoked the fire and put large pans of water to heat on top of the stove. Al went to the basement and brought up glass jars, and I washed and sterilized them for packing the tomatoes.

Al at his loom, weaving his homespun wool into wall hangings, 1977.

That fall we preserved two hundred jars of tomatoes, sixteen quarts of peaches, twenty pints of pickles, thirty quarts of string beans, eighteen quarts of spinach, forty quarts of peas, forty quarts of corn, twenty quarts of berries and thirty-five quarts of salmon. We also dried peas, beans, onions and garlic. Our root cellar was filled with carrots, turnips, rutabagas, potatoes and other root crops.

We did have a small refrigerator and a deep freezer, but they ran on kerosene. The refrigerator was very economical on fuel, but over a year the deep freezer took many barrels of kerosene, which is difficult to transport to the island. So we used the deep freezer only occasionally, when we had butchered beef or lamb.

Several days into the canning, as I moved through the beach garden cutting stems of everlasting flowers for drying over winter, Rosalind's small sailboat blew into Home Bay. "Hey Mary," she yelled. "Let's head for town for a few days for some fun. I'm tired of pickling, preserving and pestering with Bill and the kids."

It sounded great to me. Rosalind tied up her boat and we gathered up my flowers and headed to the house to make plans.

When Al came in from milking Rosie, Rosalind greeted him with, "I'm here to steal Mary away for a few days." Al laughed and yelled, "Good riddance! Where are you two heading for?"

"I have an old girl friend in Victoria who is leaving her apartment and going to South America for a trip," Rosalind answered. "She has offered me the apartment while she is away."

I took the milking bucket from Al and began to strain the milk through a cloth into jars that would fit in the refrigerator. "Will you live without me for a few days, Al?"

"What a chance for a bit of peace and quiet," was his smart remark.

I spent the next few days preparing to leave the island. I made extra loaves of bread, baked cookies and cakes, made the house quite livable and the flower gardens weed-free and well watered. Al watched me tidy things up and prepare for my leaving and finally said, "For God's sakes, Mary, you aren't going away for good, are you? I was a bachelor for thirty-nine years before I met you and got along quite handily. So leave a few things for me to keep busy with." I agreed and began to pack my bag for Victoria.

Valerie and Sharon Ryan gather oysters for breakfast. We didn't have to dress up to pick up fresh seafood on the beach at Home Bay.

Al took Rosalind and me over to French Creek on Vancouver Island, where Rosalind kept a small British car at the government dock. We were grateful the little car started right off, without coaxing. Al loaded our luggage from the boat to the car and we waved goodbye from the dock. He headed back to Jedediah before darkness fell. The day was crisp and the water calm.

Rosalind and I headed down island to Victoria, tucked snugly into the front seat of her motor car. As we motored along the scenic Malahat Drive, we admired the Gulf Islands that were silhouetted in the sea below us. "Rosalind," I said, "do you suppose the people living down there on those islands have the same joys and tribulations we have on our islands?"

"I think their lives are a bit different," she answered, "as they are fairly close to the amenities of the city, where we are very much more isolated. A lot of them have hydro power, ferry service, schools and other benefits."

It seemed to me that while we may lack these benefits, our way of life was filled with a peace and tranquility they could not experience. Our isolation also meant solitude, which brings us to a better understanding of ourselves and our part in nature's plan.

"I often think of the people in the city," I said to Rosalind as we approached Victoria. "How can they know the joys we feel when we watch the eagles teach their young to fly, or experience the birth of a new fawn in the bush, or laugh at the antics of the seals rolling down grassy knolls to the sea?"

Rosalind pointed as we drove up to a large apartment building. "Here we are," she announced. "Now if I can find where she left the key, we are home safe." Rosalind found the key under the mat. We went in, switched on the lights and felt the heat from the furnace. "Well," Rosalind remarked, "we won't be packing wood for a while." That first night we dropped quickly into bed.

Over our morning coffee we made plans. We agreed we

From a viewpoint high on Jedediah, Al and his niece Paige gaze out over Bull Island, home of our friend Rosalind Hildred, 1986.

would spend our days looking through thrift shops for necessary clothing and utensils to take back with us. We would also spend time sightseeing and visiting museums and parks. Our nights would be filled with interesting dining experiences and a few movies or plays.

The thrift shops proved to be a treasure trove of work clothes, pans and skillets, bedding and linens, and clothes for Aaron and Todd. And it was fun to shop for store-bought food. We were not accustomed to quick-cooking packaged dinners and bakery goods, so we tried to sample them all. We enjoyed finding unusual cuisine, and we ate a few dinners at ethnic restaurants.

Our most memorable evening was spent in a movie theatre, where we watched the movie *The Mosquito Coast*. We had both read the book by Paul Theroux. When it was over, Rosalind and I stayed glued to our seats, hardly believing what we had just witnessed. It was a total reenactment of her life on Bull Island. The Harrison Ford character was a duplicate of Bill, striving for a goal that was impossible, and intolerant to the needs of the people around him. Rosalind had been absolutely spellbound. "I'm living this story," she said finally. So were many other people living around Lasqueti Island, I realized. We left the theatre in wonderment.

On our last day in Victoria, we stuffed Rosalind's little British auto with our treasures and headed back to French Creek. Al was waiting on the dock when we arrived with our booty. We all unloaded the car to the boat, and headed back home. Rosalind and I had had a glorious respite, but were anxious to be home again.

The day was cool and the water still. We sped over the ten-mile trip smoothly. As we passed Sangster Island, Rosalind said, "Have you been over there during springtime? It's lovely then, just covered with wildflowers." I said that we had often intended to visit the island but never were aboard. "It seems like we always pass it in a hurry on our way home," I said. "One day we'll make a special trip just there."

Aaron and Todd heard our speedboat approach and were on the beach to greet their mother when she arrived. In between hugs and kisses, they unloaded their new things. Bill came down to the beach to greet us as we were leaving.

My friend Beverly in the kitchen at Jedediah, 1980s.

Several days later, I was out on the front verandah shaking out our lunch cloth when I noticed a sleek sailboat floating in Home Bay. I continued to wave the cloth, now trying to get the sailors' attention. Finally I caught the eye of a tall, lean fellow. I yelled, "The tide is running out on you, best if you anchor out a bit farther, near the entrance to the bay."

"I realize the tide runs out," he called, "but my boat has a double keel and can stay flat on the bottom. She will stay upright on her keel with the tide out, then float as the tide water returns."

"Fine," was my answer. "You are welcome to come ashore any time for a hike."

Before long, three people climbed down a rope boat ladder to the dry bay and walked across the tide flats to the trail up to the house. We met the boaters at our back door. Al introduced us and Carolin, who was with us for the weekend.

The older man, Barry Smith, was a tall, lithe fellow with a extremely courteous manner. His wife Edna was a small, vivacious, pretty woman with bobbed brown hair and a very pleasing personality. Their son Douglas was shy, and at an awkward stage of adolescence.

"I hope we are not intruding upon your privacy or on your time," said Barry.

Al told them it was a pleasure to have them. Edna asked if they could climb up one of our hills for exercise, as they had been aboard the boat since early that morning. We walked along with them for a while. The two dogs, Belle and Pepper, were delighted with Douglas as he raced about with them, full of energy. We took them to the orchard and showed them the best way to start up Gibraltar. The three sailors and two dogs set out to climb to the high peak.

When they returned from their hike, Al was in the garden picking the last of the beans that would be dried for winter. They all joined in to help him harvest the beans, and he dug some carrots and potatoes for them to take back home. We invited them to share our evening meal with us.

Al plowing between fruit trees in the orchard, 1980.

Recently we had butchered a fine young ram, which I had cooked with curry. We enjoyed a delicious dinner with good conversation. Barry commented that his father had been a tea merchant in India and he had been raised on curry. He did enjoy our curried lamb, but he also remarked, "Your tea is like sweepings, Mary. I must send you some proper tea." Edna mentioned she had a very good friend, Lucille Fisher, who was related to Evadne Phillips. Her stepfather was Leslie Phillips, who was active in the fishing industry. He was one of the first presidents of the BC Fishermen's Co-op, and a founding officer of the Fishermen's Co-operative Federation.

After dinner we all joined the Smiths on their fine sailboat for a nightcap. Barry, a native of Ireland, had an excellent bottle of Bushnell's aboard. He and Al tipped many toasts that evening while Edna and I enjoyed our sherry. Carolin, who was too young for alcohol, sipped cider. After a while she began to get quite bubbly and to recall many racy jokes she had heard at school, and suddenly I realized the girl was tipsy. I had been giving her generous amounts of cider, not knowing it had alcohol in it! Best we say goodnight.

Barry unfastened the dinghy and we loaded into the tiny boat. Before long we were quite anxious to reach land, so that we could relieve ourselves. As we made for the beach, Edna flashed a bright searchlight on us to help us find our way up the path. Al yelled at her to put it out as he was in distress. Quickly she got the picture and doused the light.

The Smiths sailed into Home Bay on many occasions for many years after that, making our holidays more joyous. They always brought along a "diplomatic bag" of special goodies for us. Edna was an assistant librarian at the West Vancouver Memorial Library. She would bring us books that had gone out of circulation, which she had purchased for a pittance. We were most grateful to read them and pass them on to our neighbours on Texada and Lasqueti islands. Books in winter on the coast were a treasure.

Fresh-air celebration of a youngster's birthday, with guests from Bull and Texada islands, 1986.

One Christmas Day we celebrated the holiday by hosting a dinner for our neighbours, the Joneses, Coxes, Dougans, Peter and Esther, and Christy from nearby Boo Hoo Island. (The island's real name is Boho, but after a traveller lost his rowboat and got stranded there, it was nicknamed Boo Hoo.) Everyone had arrived and the festivities were under way, when the sails of a boat appeared through the misty fog. The scene was as eerie as a surrealist painting. Everyone left the dinner table and ran to the beach to welcome Edna and Barry. They were weary, cold and hungry. Edna was almost stiff with cold. While Barry was busy anchoring the boat, we quickly took Edna up to the house. We stood her near the big wood-burning heater and gave her a hot toddy. Then we warmed up the Christmas feast and they filled their plates.

Between bites, Barry told us about their long trip. "We left Vancouver early, at dawn, for Jedediah. After an hour or two of sailing, a fog engulfed us. I had set the course before the fog arrived and I also fastened an aluminum pie tin to the mast, to help other ships spot us. We could not see farther than a foot ahead of us. It's a miracle, but here we are." Everyone joined in a toast congratulating them for a successful sail.

Our after-dinner conversation was filled with tales of harrowing experiences on the sea during foggy or stormy weather. To our delight, the Smiths stayed several days. Many of our other guests stayed overnight, as the light fades so early on winter days. Christy, the Joneses, and Peter and Esther left together the next morning. Peter and Esther lived in Boom Bay on Jedediah, and the Joneses dropped Christy off on Boo Hoo Island on their way home to Lasqueti.

Peter and Esther were Americans—she from New York and he from the south—who had migrated to Lasqueti during the mid-1960s and joined the other young people of the area, in search of peace and love. Together they had built a float house and kept it anchored in Boom Bay. They raised a fine garden and helped us with chores on Jedediah. Finally, after seven years, they bought property on Lasqueti and moved to their own land.

While I was still writing for the *Seattle Times*, I sent them an article giving an account of our life on Jedediah during the winter months of the 1970s.

Big Red with his cock-a-doodle-doo announced the new day. Only a glimmer of light filtered through the limbs of the giant Douglas fir trees. I fumbled for my flashlight. How I regretted leaving the warmth of the flannel sheets. Puff, the cat, leaped out first to show me the way downstairs to her empty food pan. The old wooden steps creaked and groaned as I made my way down the stairs.

I struck a match and touched it to the wick of the kerosene lamp. The glow showed me the stack of dry kindling in the oven of the cooking stove. Lighting the fireplace took a bit more skill. Rumpled paper, fine oven-dried kindling and a few small pieces of dry alder, and away it went.

I went outdoors and splashed a bit of cold water from a bucket over my face and hands.

"More snow and gale warnings for the straits," was the weather report on the battery-operated radio. This brought down Al, the man of the house.

"Where are my hip waders? I better get out to check the lines on the boat, with a storm coming up."

Emptying last night's coffee grounds, I washed the pot outdoors by the water pump and refilled it. Buckets of water by the pump had a thin film of ice over them. My wash basin had refrozen already.

Soon the coffee was perking and the bacon spread

thinly in the bottom of a black iron frying pan was crisp.

By this time, Al had opened the kitchen door to go down to the boat. First to push through the door were Belle and Pepper, our two farm dogs. They swiftly settled in behind the stove.

Al had returned from securing the boat's anchor lines and was ready for breakfast.

"What's your choice this morning?" I asked Al. "Duck, goose, guinea or chicken eggs?"

"Don't get smart, just scramble your usual conglomeration," was his reply.

Eight o'clock, time to switch on the citizen's-band radio. Turning the dial to No. 11, the call station, I called, "Fulton Bay, Fulton Bay, Jedediah calling."

A male voice answered. "Fulton Bay here, let's go to channel 5." Quickly turning to channel 5, I inquired: "How many eggs did those birds lay yesterday, Bill?"

"Enough."

"Did Gertrude, the stubborn old goat, butt Billy out of the shed last night in the storm?"

"No, Gert is a lady, she knows how to behave."

A familiar voice cut in with: "Top of the morning to you all."

"You listening in, Jim? Have you downed those famous sourdough pancakes yet? What leftovers did you toss into the dough this morning, a couple of old fish heads?"

"Oh, you folks are all jealous of an inventive cook, so I'll sign off and finish up the last of my pancakes."

"Texada clear, back to channel 11."

"Fulton Bay clear," was heard and I chimed in with, "Jedediah clear, back to channel 11."

"Hey, don't sign off yet, this is Christy from Boo

Hoo Island, Mary. I'll row over today to your Deep Bay if weather permits and walk through the trail. I need more wool to finish knitting my boot socks."

"Great, Christy," I answered. "See you later. Jedediah back to channel 11."

"Boo Hoo back to channel 11."

A few weeks after the Christmas holidays we were sitting in front of the fireplace with a cup of coffee when Al said, "What's first on the list of chores for today, old girl?"

"Better repair the chicken house. Some of the support beams are sagging and the wire is missing in some spots. We are lucky that hungry mink, raccoon and other fowl lovers haven't made nocturnal visits to the hen house lately."

Before leaving the house with the repairman, I set a batch of bread and stoked up the fires with heavy bark.

Al taking a break from cutting firewood. The wood pile shown here was just about enough for one winter on Jedediah.

Walking out to the chicken house I heard a faint *baa, baa* and on the ground I found two wee black woolly lambs. Our yearling ewe was the mother of twins. The two stood on their wobbly legs and found the milk spigots. Tails and backsides wiggled wildly as they fed.

Repairs to the chicken pen were delayed. I called to Al, as the newborns needed our attention. We led the mother into the barn to a warm pen, with the two new ones following. Al gave the nursing ewe some extra grain and fresh alfalfa. We watched them for a while, then headed out to see if any more lambs were being born, but we found no other new ones.

We went to the beach to prowl about in search of building lumber, cedar logs to split for shakes, or odd pieces that we could use in repairs or new projects.

Amazing how much workable material floats in on a high, windy tide. Along with logs and lumber come old brooms, hats, mops, grapefruits, oranges, plastic dishpans, shoes and buckets by the bushel.

Out in the bay at the tideline, the sleek head of a hair seal bobbed up to watch us. These curious creatures follow a boat more closely when dogs are aboard and the outboard motor is turned off. Sometimes when I am out fishing, they stay alongside the boat, as if to land the fish first.

As we were pulling lumber up from the beach, Christy appeared. In heavy rubber gumboots, she walked with an awkward gait. Only the tips of her long, braided brown hair showed beneath her home-knitted cap. A woolly turtleneck sweater covered her throat, and over all she was clothed in a tentlike raincoat, which billowed behind her. We went to meet her and take her up through the orchard to the house for lunch. Al started a blazing fire in the cook stove and fireplace while I rustled up lunch for us.

After lunch Al went back outside to work on the chicken

house. Christy and I cozied up by the fireplace to enjoy our tea, and I asked her how she had found caretaking Boo Hoo.

She smiled. "I was in my third year of college in Portland and summer vacation time was near," she said. "I needed a summer job. On the college bulletin board was a notice for a caretaker on a Canadian island. I contacted Dr. and Mrs. Nichols and here I am. I wanted just a summertime job, but found living on Boo Hoo longer was to my liking. I know I have to return to college to get my degree, but in the meantime my life here is wonderful. I'll probably go back to school next fall." She pulled a large basket of wool skeins near us and we began sorting them out as we talked.

"The Nicholses really lucked out when they found you," I said. "He has had quite a few losers for caretakers. Ruth and Rob, the ones before you, were excellent, but Rob and Dr. Nichols didn't enjoy each other's company and by the end of last summer they were quite hostile. You know how to handle the old codger, by keeping him on his toes, not bending to his every whim, and standing your ground. I believe he admires a free thinker and has no use for a person who bows to his wishes. Underneath his outside attitude is hidden a good soul. He loves life on the coast and is giving his family experiences they would never enjoy if he wasn't around. Did your dad ever practise medicine with Dr. Nichols?"

"They know each other, but Dad is a cancer specialist and Dr. Nichols is a hand and foot surgeon, and a very good one."

We finished our tea and worked on the wool skeins. Al had spun them from our sheep's wool, then we had dyed the wool with lichens, mosses, walnut shells, bark, onion skins, leaves and other materials from the island. So we had many natural colours for Christy to choose from. Al found spinning to be an enjoyable evening hobby, while I knitted our sweaters, caps, shawls, gloves and socks. Most of our wool creations went to friends and relatives.

"Have you seen the Joneses lately?" I asked Christy.

"Yes, they check up on me often as we live so close to each other. I sometimes give them a hand with their oyster culture business. They take me to town often, when they take a load of oysters in to the market. Often they drive down to Seattle and I go along and visit my folks in Portland."

"I know you miss your family," I said.

"Yes, at times," she answered. She was Jewish and she missed the deep, rich culture, the music and art. "Yet I find my life here is also fulfilling. I have time to do a lot of reading and reevaluating my goals for the future. There is a special peace and tranquility I find in the isolation of the islands."

I added another thick piece of dry bark to the fireplace. We looked up through the tall, narrow windows and noticed the day was beginning to end.

Christy gathered her wool skeins into her backpack and tossed her tentlike raincoat over her shoulders. "It was a great afternoon, Mary," she said. "These breaks keep me going."

"Me too, Christy. Come over again soon. Next time we'll get busy and bake up a storm. Will you show me how to make bagels?"

"Next time, Mary. See you soon."

Christy had picked a calm, sunny winter's day for visiting. The next morning we awoke to the sound of the wind tormenting the sea. Gusts of wind pounded the waves against the jagged black rocks of the shoreline. We thought of our boat immediately.

Al pushed down the path against the wind to the beach. He untied the small skiff from the dock and made his way to the boat. The anchor lines were secured tightly and the line from boat to beach was checked. The boat was held secure. It was a relief. Often during a stormy night your thoughts go wild, as you envision the lines of your boat coming loose, and the craft dashed to pieces against the rocks. Next we made our way to the barn to check on the new lambs and calves. All was well. The winds of March were upon us. A perfect day for a warm, cozy time indoors by the fire with our favourite books.

In that same season, an eclipse of the sun occurred. It was announced for several weeks, and Al was ecstatic. He installed a satellite dish so that we could watch the phenomenon on television. We invited the entire neighbourhood to watch with us, and I prepared brunch for us all. Bill Cox, his Margaret, Jim Dougan, Peter, Esther, Loretta, her friend Darrell, and the Farrell family all attended. If only Jenny and Jimmy could be here to witness the event, I thought. At the turn of the century, Jedediah could only boast a few battery-operated radios. Now we had TV. Imagine such an advance of technology, that could bring images and sounds to a remote island.

The eclipse was spectacular. Reception via the new TV dish was loud and clear. To me the strangest part of the event was after the sky had gone completely dark, then a slit of light returned—and our roosters crowed as if it were the dawning of a new day.

Several days later the *Vulture* drifted into Home Bay, and Sam leaned out of the wheelhouse and yelled, "Get the frying pan on, Mary! I landed a few bluebacks." Anne waved her greeting and they both piled into the skiff and made their way to shore. By the time they had reached the kitchen door, I had the potatoes peeled and Al had run down to the root cellar and brought up some vegetables. We all savoured our lunch from the sea and soil.

As we ate, Sam told us of a plan by BC Hydro to build huge power cables and towers. The first towers would be constructed near Pender Harbour. An underwater cable would be built and laid on the ocean floor, then rise again to gigantic towers over

Jedediah and Lasqueti, then down under water again to reach Vancouver Island.

This would mean a right-of-way of one and a half miles of destruction, leaving no trees, other vegetation, no nothing but electric currents on towers and lines ninety feet in the air.

We were all in shock.

"What can be done to stop this?" Al asked.

"That is one reason we came over to see you," Sam answered. "A meeting at the community hall is planned for tomorrow. We hoped you would come along too."

"You bet we'll be there," was my reply.

"Maybe it's best if you come along today. Follow the *Vulture* in your boat, and stay overnight with us. The weather could be rough tomorrow and I believe it's imperative you attend this meeting."

Sam and Al went to get the boat ready while Anne and I tidied up the kitchen and made certain the fires were extinguished. I

Texada Island, as seen from the back garden at Home Bay.

packed an overnight case and we left for the boats.

The *Vulture* ploughed through the sea ahead of us. We crossed the Sabine Channel, passed by Fulton Bay on Texada Island and on through the Malaspina Strait, into Pender Harbour on the mainland. We tied up to Sam's dock in front of their new home. The sky was beginning to darken, with threatening clouds above. Al looked skyward and remarked, "Good thing we came over tonight, looks like a storm brewing."

The next day the community hall overflowed with concerned citizens. Many spoke out vehemently against the project, noting the destruction of wildlife habitat and the devastation of the pristine land. The people rallied around to defeat the plan, and the project was abandoned. Disaster had been averted. Later, a new technology made it possible for BC Hydro to lay a workable cable beneath the sea without disturbing the land.

After a day or two we returned to Jedediah, confident that the island was to remain undisturbed.

The evening we arrived home, Bill Cox called on the CB radiophone from Texada and asked if we would like to come along with him and Margaret over the hill and on to Vananda, near the north end of Texada. Al accepted the invitation.

Before dawn, Al and I motored over to Bill's homestead at Fulton Bay. Al decided to set an anchor far out into the bay as the tide would be out by the time we returned that night. "Jump out quickly," he told me, "while I take her out deeper." I jumped out of the boat onto a slippery, rocky outcropping. Al anchored out with a long line, then he pulled himself into shore by the rope that was tied to shore.

We walked up a woodland trail approximately a quarter of a mile to Bill and Margaret's home. A hand-split cedar fence guarded the well-kept flower garden near their home, and a herd of goats greeted us at the gate. Their cottage was cozy and small. We entered through a large enclosed porch at the back that

Margaret Boyer and Bill Cox, friends from Texada Island, 1974. They hosted an unforgettable weekend-long barbecue in late August every year.

was a combination store-room and entry hall. Along one wall, sacks of animal feed were piled high. Shelves were filled with sundries and staples necessary for isolated island living. Hanging high from the rafters was an assortment of dried fish, sausage and deer jerky. The aromas were wondrous.

At the doorway to the kitchen Bill greeted us with, "Top of the morning to you. Have a quick cup of coffee with us before we leave."

Margaret had decorated the former bachelor quarters with a warm country style. She had made chintz curtains to cover the open shelves of dishes, pots and pans that lined the kitchen walls. Tapestries and pictures hung on the parlour walls. The open bedroom closets were draped in bright fabrics. Bill was proud of her improvements.

We finished our coffee and went outdoors to the waiting Jeep. Bill's brother Gordon, who was still logging up coast, had brought Bill this old Jeep, and other logging equipment for use on the ranch. So Bill was no longer dependent on the sea and boats to transport his supplies. The Jeep made it possible to drive to the north end of Texada for animal feed, groceries and other necessities.

Margaret was last to step out of the cottage onto a board

walkway and jump into the Jeep. Bill fired up the vehicle and we took off, dodging a group of goats.

The Jeep roared up an old logging road. The deep ruts in the road, caused by rushing water from rains, gave us all jumps and jolts. After three or four miles we came to a sign in the road announcing the appropriately named Break Your Ass Hill. Bill had logged the area in the '40s and '50s, so he was familiar with the terrain, this hill particularly. He gunned the engine and made a run for it. The tires shrieked and squealed as the wheels spun up the steep grade. Stark terror gave way to relief as we reached the top, where we found a flat pastoral scene.

Texada is made up of igneous rock—rock that has been produced by heat and pressure. The area is high and more rugged than Jedediah, with deeper shorelines and fewer safe anchorages. The south end of the island is exposed to the southeast and unprotected from strong gales.

"How about stopping here for lunch?" Bill shouted back to us.

We spread our lunch basket out on a mossy knoll, placing ourselves near a ledge where we could admire the view. Bill pointed out the entrance to Pender Harbour, and the top of Mount Baker to the south. We were awed by the magnificent scenery and the solitude.

I strolled along the hill to check out the native plants. "Look at the bunch of gentians growing here," I said. "We must be very high—they usually thrive in mountainous areas over 5,000 feet." Nearby were a few kalmias bunched together with violets at their feet.

After lunch Bill started up the Jeep and we continued our excursion. We rambled along the rough road until we came to a wide, straight, well-paved highway. We had reached civilization.

Our first stop in the coastal village of Vananda was the feed store. Bill picked up a few sacks of goat and chicken feed and Al

Looking across Sabine Channel to Texada Island, as an Alaskan cruise ship passes through.

tossed in three or four bags of grain for the cows, sheep and chickens. Our next port of call was the town's one and only grocery store. Margaret and I eagerly searched the shelves for tea, coffee, flour, sugar, spices—and, for us "girls," exotic treats such as special tinned biscuits from England and chocolates from Belgium. We were truly like two kids loose in a candy store. Our next stop was the hotel and coffee shop for an early dinner before returning home.

We rumbled back to Fulton Bay just before dusk. We unloaded Bill's supplies, then he ran the Jeep down to the beach where we could load our feed and groceries. Al and I waved goodbye, thanking Bill and Margaret for a most wonderful experience. We had often gazed at Texada's high terrain, never imagining we would reach the other end of the island by road, over impossible mountain passes.

While we were trekking over Texada, Chris Brand had come over to check our livestock and milk Rosie, the cow. Chris and her husband David were a young couple who lived at one end of

Jedediah, at Long Bay. They had built a small cabin, and David ran a tugboat named the *Wee Geordie*. To pay for his use of the land, David brought us drums of kerosene and gas. He also made a fair living hauling freight for people in the area, and Chris took care of our animals when we left the island.

In 1977 both Chris and Margaret Dougan, on Texada, were pregnant. The only doctor in the area at the time was practicing on Lasqueti. He made a call to Chris on Jedediah and advised her to go to Nanaimo immediately for the birth of her baby. She did so. He then sailed over to Texada to visit Margaret, and advised her to leave for the hospital at Pender Harbour. No way—Jim Dougan wanted a home birth. So be it. Dr. Paul, who lived on Lasqueti, stayed with the Dougans for three or four days awaiting the arrival of the new one. Finally a tiny girl was born at the Dougan home. She was named Tilly.

Chris and David became the parents of Rebecca, and a year and a half later they were blessed with another girl, Kathleen. The family stayed on Jedediah for two or three years, until a fierce winter storm blew out their windows and frightened Chris terribly.

At the height of the storm, David was in French Creek, stormbound at the dock after picking up supplies. We were awakened in the middle of the night by screams of "Help me, help me!" at our back door. When Al ran down the stairs and opened the door, he found Chris standing outside, rain-drenched, with baby Kathleen in her arms and Rebecca hanging tight to her mother's skirts.

By then I was in the kitchen. Immediately we started up a fire in the stove, which had copper pipes in the firebox to heat water and carry it to a tank at the back of the stove. I filled a teacup half full of rye whisky, added boiling water to it and gave the hot toddy to Chris. We put the little ones near the fire and gave them hot chocolate. As soon as the water was hot, I filled our bathtub and put Chris and the young ones into the water. They shivered and shook until they were soaking warmly in the tub.

Al opened our sofa bed in the parlour and made it up with warm flannel sheets and comforters. He built up the fire in the heating stove in the parlour and added dry chunks of bark to bank the fire for the night. After their bath, we made sure the terrorized three were safe in bed.

David and Chris Brand and their children, 1980. They lived at Long Bay on Jedediah.

The next morning Chris was still devastated. "Mary," she said, "you'll never know how strong the wind howled through the trees. Branches were falling all around us and I had no flashlight to see where we were. Good thing I had travelled the trail so many times before. We fell and climbed over fallen trees and branches, then into deep gullies in the ground. I know our little house is blown to pieces by now."

After breakfast Al and I helped Chris and the girls back to their home at Long Bay, making our way slowly by climbing over fallen logs and debris from the storm. Their little home had endured—all but the kitchen windows. Al put the broken frames back in place and covered them with pieces of plywood, until David could put in new glass.

A few weeks after the storm, Chris declared she had had enough of pioneering with two little ones. They moved the family to Ladysmith, near Nanaimo. Chris returned to school and in a few years was working as a teacher. David continued working with the *Wee Geordie* at the mill in Ladysmith.

"Today seems like the day for me to go fishing," I announced one morning. "Our supply of salmon is down to three jars."

Al wanted the day to clear more fields for the animals to graze, but I longed to fish. I gathered my fishing gear and made for the rowboat. Belle followed me but Pepper, who was shy of water and boats, wandered out to the fields to be with Al.

I untied the lines, took off my dry socks and shoes and climbed aboard barefoot into our "gone leaky" rowboat. Belle found her place near the bow. The rowing oars squeaked against the oarlocks. I pulled strongly through the kelp beds out to where I knew were the feeding grounds for our underwater prey. The tide and the wind were a match for my rowing.

I put out two fish lines rigged with lures and rowed toward the waterfall on the west side of Texada, where fish fed. I rowed up and down the area, and at one turn the left line gave a jerk. Quickly I reeled in the right line and kept the left line taut, then let out a bit of line for the fish to play. I played out more line, then gave the line a stiff jerk and slowly reeled it in.

Alongside the boat, my fish fought. I could see a spot on the upper half of the tailfin which told me it was a coho or a blueback (a coho in its second year of life).

If I touched the tail it would be "game over." I reached for the landing net, carefully scooped up the thrashing fish and landed it into the boat. Belle yelped wildly all the while. I took the blunt end of the oar and put an end to the fish's misery. Then I removed the hook from its mouth and laid it along the bottom of the boat.

My bare feet were submerged in water that had seeped into the boat. I had been bailing it out slowly with a pail, but I knew it would be best to turn the boat over on its side and let all the water run out. Also I wanted to give Belle a run and stretch my legs. I rowed to shore.

As we walked along the beach, we heard a rustling in the bush and a doe made an appearance. She stood about three and a half feet high, with her large ears held upright. Her coat was a reddish-buff colour and she had white patches on her

Carolin with a day's catch. Fishing was always a satisfying day out at Jedediah.

throat and rump. She was feeding on salal and dwarf huckleberry plants. When she became aware of Belle and me, she turned and showed a whitish tail tipped with black, then darted back into the bush with a "bouncing ball" gait, all four feet coming down together with the front feet before the hind feet.

I kept Belle close to my side to avoid any chase. After our walk, I took a sandwich and thermos out of the boat and enjoyed a bit of lunch. Belle had a chew on a bone I had packed along. While lunching, I watched flocks of seagulls feeding near the surface of the water. Every once in a while an eagle swooped down from its perch high above us, took a fish with its strong talons and returned to its perch.

Time to put the rowboat back in the water. Belle jumped in and took her place. I reset the tackle, put out two lines behind the boat, fastened the poles to the sides and continued to row.

All around us seabirds scurried on top of the water, scooping up small fishes.

I rowed slowly into the frenzy. Both my poles were bending under the weight of another strike. Quickly I reached for the right one and it gave a hard tug—then nothing. I had lost one. I reeled in the line, then unfastened the other pole from the side of the boat and held it tightly in my hand. When I felt a strong tug, I played the fish by giving out more line, then pulling with a jerk to set the hook. I had him. Now to net and bring him into the boat.

Belle and I fished for another hour or two, and brought in our limit. I was very careful to take only our limit, as during the height of fishing season there were many fishery inspectors cruising around these isolated islands. Just the previous week Rosalind had been out in her boat fishing and had caught several undersized salmon, called "grilse." Suddenly she noticed an inspector's boat speeding near her. Quickly she stuffed the fish down the front of her blouse. Had the officer seen them, she risked a big fine, and confiscation of her boat and tackle. Rosalind squirmed about, but was successful in hiding her catch. After the officer's boat was out of sight, she removed the fish, washed out her blouse over the side of the boat, and continued to fish.

I pulled the oars strongly and headed home toward Jedediah. The sun was still high, my spirits soared and I broke out in song, much to Belle's dismay. The louder I sang the more frantically she raised her head and howled.

When we reached Home Bay the tide was out. I jumped out of the boat and pulled it in as far as I could toward the beach. I put a long line and light anchor out. The incoming tide would wash the boat in toward the beach if I gave it plenty of line.

Our new neighbours Loretta and Darrell were in our orchard picking apples when I returned from my fishing excursion. Loretta was originally from Alberta and Darrell from the States. They had moved into the cabin that the Brands had left, in Long Bay. Loretta was a skilled weaver, and she often worked with our wool and helped at shearing time. She became quite successful at weaving and sold some of her art work throughout Canada and the States. I invited the

Al shearing sheep with two young helpers, 1980s.

two of them in and we all enjoyed a fresh fish dinner and the pleasure of each other's company. It was the perfect end to another beautiful day on Jedediah.

Chapter

5

IN THE 1970S I WAS STILL RETURNING OFTEN to Seattle to deliver my articles to the *Seattle Times*, and on these occasions I would give talks to schools or gardening groups. One afternoon in 1976 I gave a garden talk to the students of the Kent Meridian High School, near Seattle, and I found that the teachers and students were more intrigued by the lifestyle on Jedediah Island than they were by gardening. After the talk, we discussed the possibility of some of the teachers and students visiting us on Jedediah. They continued to make plans, and finally they made their trip.

They travelled to Vancouver Island first. At French Creek they boarded the ferry boat *Captain Vancouver* for Lasqueti Island. We met them at False Bay on Lasqueti, with our old open truck. We drove them right to the other end of Lasqueti, about twelve miles along a dirt road, to Squitty Bay, where we had moored our boat. We loaded ten people aboard the boat and headed for Jedediah.

Al gave a hands-on demonstration of weaving, sheep shearing and milking a temperamental milk cow. Then most of them rode out into the fields and helped Al cut alders to clear more grazing land. The students cut the logs into chunks and loaded

The garden path, 1987.

the wood onto a small wagon. Will, our horse, hauled the wood to the shed. Some of the girls enjoyed making butter from the fresh cream. Cheese and bread were priorities. The three days they stayed on Jedediah were filled with challenges and chores. Al and I will always have wonderful memories of the people from Kent Meridian High School.

Will, our wonderful horse, had been brought to Jedediah in precarious conditions. Peter had kept Will as a riding horse on Lasqueti after the animal had been brought over in the late 1960s with several other horses on the open ferry *Captain Vancouver*. Will was the only stallion, having sired many foals running freely on Lasqueti, then having been castrated to prevent an overpopulation of horses there. Our grandchildren Carolin, Sally and Andy were longing for a horse to ride, so Peter suggested we barge Will from Lasqueti to Jedediah. Al and Peter built a small barge, with a box in the centre to keep

Will steady. We planned to tow the barge with our motorboat. A veterinarian gave us a tranquilizer in a syringe to give Will before the sea voyage.

Al, Peter and Carolin picked a calm, windless day for the trip. They arrived on Lasqueti early in the morning and got a lead rope on Will, who was in a pasture near Squitty Bay, our point of departure.

Also in the bay were several tourist boats from which some curious people watched the proceedings. One sailboat had a crew of local people and guests from

Al rides our old horse Will through the fields he cleared, 1978. Will sired a good many horses on Lasqueti Island before being barged carefully to Jedediah, which is still his home.

a ranch in Alberta. The cowboy from Alberta was a great help. He understood the problem of getting a horse to walk onto a moving object such as a dock, to a plank, to a moving barge.

Between his scotch and sodas, he advised us to moor the boat near the beach, where the horse could be coaxed to the barge easier. He gave the horse the tranquilizer, then a hefty slap on the rump, and Will made it into the pen on the barge. Peter stayed near the horse and rubbed his ears. The cowboy kept yelling, "Hey fella, talk to the horse, keep talking to the horse."

Peter was doing his best. The tranquilizer began to take effect and Will settled in. Al started the motor on the boat, and made his way out of Squitty Bay, barge in tow, when a bit of wind started up.

Peter kept talking to Will as the caravan made its way toward Jedediah. The trip was only two or three miles, but towing a sleepy horse behind the boat made the trip seem endless.

When a northerly wind beat against the barge, Al slowed the boat to a snail's pace. Peter and Will were weathering the trip pretty well, even when they reached the opening of Home Bay and Will thrust one hoof through the bottom of the barge. Al swung the boat into Home Bay near a low, sandy beach. They beached the barge and let Will out. Everyone rejoiced.

Since then, Al, our visitors and all our grandchildren have ridden and enjoyed Will. Jedediah has been his home for more than twenty-three years now. He is a part of Jedediah and will remain so for many more years.

Mail day brought a letter from Elda Mason, a former resident of Lasqueti Island and author of an excellent, informative book on Lasqueti, *Lasqueti Island, History and Memory*, as well as an updated and revised edition. She wrote that she was planning a visit that summer, to attend Cedric Hawkshaw's picnic.

I plan to stay with Molly Millicheap and to go to Cedric Hawkshaw's picnic, and the rest is an "if and a hope."

You once so kindly invited me to visit you on Jedediah. At the time I thought I might get there with my son and his boat, but so far he is too busy. But I have had the thought that if you come to Cedric's on the 30th, and if the invitation is still open, perhaps I could go back with you to Jedediah for a visit.

I know this may not be convenient for you or the weather maybe unwilling, or you might have other plans or not be able to get back to Lasqueti. So please let me know, and I'll understand if this plan is not feasible.

You probably heard that my husband passed away in January. So I keep myself very busy, as it's the best thing to do. I garden and visit and try to keep up with things in general. My youngest son is getting married in July, so there are many events to keep me going. I'll close for now and I hope you are both keeping well.

I wrote to Elda, inviting her to Jedediah. We looked forward to her visit.

Cedric's get-together was a success. He was an excellent host. His coat of arms from England, which dates back to Thomas Hawkshaw, 1375, is inscribed with the word "Perseverance"—truly the correct motto for Cedric. He has persevered on Lasqueti for many years.

He had first arrived on the island when he was ten years old. In 1934 he and his father John were riding in a democrat pulled by one horse when the animal bolted and the democrat tumbled down a ravine, with John and son aboard. John held his son in his arms, which saved the boy. Young Cedric only had a broken arm, but his father perished.

Cedric and his mother moved away from the island after the accident, but returned often to visit. Eventually Cedric retired, and he moved back to the island permanently in the 1960s. He is a charming, sociable fellow and a fine citizen of Lasqueti. His accomplishments include the formation of the Lasqueti Historical Society in 1976. Each winter the society had a dinner banquet. A special one was held on November 21, 1981, to celebrate the 100th anniversary of early settler homesteading. Our entire family attended, along with the Mann and Ryan families, Margaret and Bill from Texada; Rosalind, Aaron and Todd from Bull Island, Christy from Boo Hoo, the Jones family from Skerry

Bay on Lasqueti, and many of the homesteaders' children and grandchildren. It was a grand affair, at which many pioneers gave vivid accounts of living before and through the depression years on Lasqueti and the surrounding islands. Some compared the lifestyle of the 1920s through the 1950s, to the invasion of the flower children and American draft dodgers in the 1960s. After the First World War, many veteran servicemen came to these islands to recover from the ravages of war. Two shell-shocked vets built a log cabin on Jedediah and lived there for a few years. At the height of the Great Depression, the Canadian government gave land, farming equipment, fruit trees and farm animals to people from the cities who were willing to migrate to isolated regions to make a go of it in the bush. Many energetic families took advantage of the offer and settled in these remote islands.

Reluctantly, Elda and Al and I took our leave of Cedric's picnic. We jumped into our pickup truck, left Cedric's ranch, drove down to Squitty Bay, boarded our boat and headed for Jedediah.

Darkness fell over the water as we travelled. Shimmering phosphorescence in the night water illuminated our pathway through the channel into Home Bay. The tide was high. Al

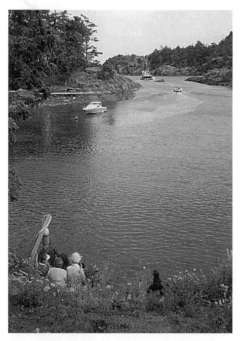

Friends cheer on Ron Mann as he departs in his fish boat, Home Bay, 1987.

helped Elda and me disembark onto the beach. He returned the boat to the middle of the bay to moor it out, and returned in the small dinghy.

As we stumbled up the path to the house, Elda remarked that she hadn't been on Jedediah since she was a small child. In the darkness of the kitchen, I struck a match and

Ron Mann's children, Debbie, Shannon, René and Sheryl, 1990.

held it to the Aladdin lamp. It glowed. The oven was filled with dry kindling to start the cook stove and heater in the parlour.

Al soon bounced in through the kitchen door. Taking off his hat and coat, he suggested we have a nightcap to celebrate Elda's return to Jedediah. He reached for his bottle of Black Label Scotch, and I brewed a pot of "mountain tea," a wild mint that grows well on the hills of Jedediah. As we sipped our drinks, we spoke of the stories we had heard that day—stories of the old days that sparked my interest and brought me back to the islands.

Someone had retold the story of Sidney Ryan cleaning out a deer and leaving the remains in the front seat of Ralph Lewis's truck. Someone else remembered when everyone heard the RCMP were coming over to check truck and car licences, and the rumour drove many a vehicle deep into the bush, out of sight.

"I remember the time Ian Cole asked me to take the wheel of the *Captain Vancouver* as the 'devil drink' had about done him in for this trip. I took the wheel of the boat and almost landed on the rocks outside the bay at Qualicum. Finally I righted the ship and found French Creek. Those ferry trips were an adventure."

I refilled Elda's mountain tea. "Do you remember the old chesterfields in the salon?" I asked. "Many a time I have shared them with a milk goat or two as passengers."

I also asked her whether she knew any more about a burglary and murder done by two fellows named Wagner and Julian. I could recall folks talking about the 1912 shooting at Union Bay. As the story went, the two of them had been pirating coastal towns for several years. During a burglary at Union Bay on Vancouver Island, a policeman was killed. They hid out on Lasqueti, and a resident of Davis Bay swore he overheard them making plans to bury their treasures there. The eavesdropper spent the whole summer digging up the beach area in search of the treasure, with no bounty. "Did you ever hear what happened to the two pirates?" I asked.

"Yes," she said. "Wagner went to the hangman's noose and Julian to the 'crowbar hotel.'"

I remarked that buried treasure has always intrigued island people, and asked Elda what she knew about the legend of buried treasure left by the Spanish looters escaping from a British cutter in the eighteenth century. The treasure was supposedly buried at the foot of Trematon Mountain, near the south end of Lasqueti.

"I found reference to it while researching my book on Lasqueti," she said. "Maybe some lucky farmer will find it while ploughing his fields."

By now, Al's head was bobbing up and down with sleep. "Come, Elda," I said, "let me show you your room." I took her and her luggage up the stairway to the west bedroom, opened the bed for her and placed in it a large stone that had been heated on the stove, then wrapped in newspapers and cloth to keep her warm for the night.

Then I returned to the parlour and tapped Al on the shoulder. "Come on, fella," I said, "let's call it a night."

Al was first down the stairs in the morning. He put the kettle on, then yelled up at me to get going, as the best part of the day was going fast. Elda had silently found her way out of doors before we arose. As I arrived in the kitchen, she met me with a handful of wildflowers. She seemed to cherish all living things, especially native plants.

Elda Copley Mason, author of *Lasqueti Island: History and Memory*, wearing her special berry-picking hat, woven from salal, 1980.

After breakfast Elda and I took a hike around the different bays of Jedediah. We hiked first to an area near Deep Bay, which looks across to Lasqueti. "This is where my dad and I crossed in a small rowboat during summer days," Elda reminisced, "to visit the Foote family and later the Hugheses who lived here at the time." She remembered that she had been quite small at the time, and that the trip across the water had been quite an adventure.

While she was reminiscing, Elda picked a few salal leaves and wove them together to fashion a hat. She started weaving the crown first, then worked down to made a wide brim. She created one for me and one for herself. As she worked patiently, she said, "You know, Mary, I used to make these in summer when we were out picking wild berries in the hot sun, to give us shade for our heads."

News of any visitor to the islands brings many people together. On this occasion, Bill and Margaret Cox and the Dougan family from Texada sailed over to spend time with Elda. As we talked together, we found out that Bill Cox and Jim Dougan were related to Elda by marriage—one of Bill's nephews had married Elda's granddaughter.

Elda stayed on Jedediah a few days. Then we returned her to the Millicheap home on Lasqueti, to continue her island sojourn.

On our way along the dirt road home from the Millicheaps', we stopped by to visit Shirley Mann and her flock. Wesley, now ten years old, Norman, Merl (who was born on Lasqueti in 1964) and Carol, the youngest girl, were with Shirley. The teenaged children had moved near Nanaimo to attend middle schools and the older boys were working on fish boats for the Forbes and Millicheaps Fish Company of Lasqueti. Soon these boys—Dan, Ron, Alfie and Vern—had boats of their own.

Cedric Hawkshaw was at Shirley's picking up a gallon of fresh milk when we arrived. To provide for her family, Shirley operated a taxi on Lasqueti. She also kept a few milk cows for the young ones and sold extra milk for a bit of cash. As soon as Cedric saw us drive up, he jumped out of his

Shirley Mann, my friend Mary Thompson, and me, 1989.

vehicle and walked over. "I didn't have a chance to tell you at the picnic," he told us, "that a couple of weeks ago I went to town to try to locate any family members of Lasqueti or Jedediah homesteaders. I found a Roy Jelly, a member of the Foote family, in White Rock, BC. Also contacted George Gurr in Surrey, BC, a nephew of Jenny Hughes. Her other nephew, Leonard Thomson, returned to England after living a few years on Jedediah."

I was amazed at Cedric's efforts to locate these people. "Cedric, we can't thank you enough for finding them," I said. "I have been searching to find anyone who knows the history of Jedediah, especially any descendants of the Foote or Hughes families. You have given me a great start."

Before the summer faded, Cedric had planned another special get-together for the descendants of the pioneers and homesteaders from the area. We notified the Foote, Olmstead and Jelly families of the event, inviting them for a visit to Jedediah at the same time.

We met the Jedediah homestead descendants at the ferry at False Bay on Lasqueti, then drove them to Cedric's for a wine and cheese social. Many brought special homemade wine, and I brought rounds of homemade cheese. Local people from Lasqueti also attended the social. Everyone had a high time reminiscing together about old days.

In the late afternoon we left Cedric's and headed for our boat, which was moored at Squitty Bay. Thelma (Jelly) Pohl of Osoyoos, BC; Alma (Olmstead) Trott of Surrey, BC; Dorothy (Olmstead) Biggs of Maple Ridge, BC; and Harry and Zella Olmstead of Courtenay, BC joined us aboard the boat. Many members of our family were on shore at Jedediah to greet us: our older son Roger and his wife Rachel, our younger son Evan and his wife Mary, and our three grandchildren, Carolin, Sally and Andy.

The get-together of friends, neighbours and descendants of
Jedediah's first white pioneers, 1978. Back row, left to right: Harry
Olmstead, Mary Mattice (Evan's wife), Shirley Mann. Middle row:
Zella Olmstead, Dorothy (Olmstead) Biggs, Alma (Olmstead) Trott,
me. Front row: Evan, Thelma (Jelly) Pohl, Carolin, Merl Mann and
our Texada Island friend Lisa Farrell.

We all enjoyed the visit of the children of the Foote family.
We spent our days hiking to familiar scenes of their childhood.
Thelma and I had a swimming race across the stretch of water
from the shore by the house, across Home Bay to the shore on
Sandy Beach. We hiked Gibraltar and added our names to the
glass jar on the highest peak. In the evenings we chatted and
they reflected on their times on Jedediah.

One special evening by the fire, Alma shared with us all her
childhood memories of Jedediah and her grandparents. "I am so
pleased to be sitting in the home that my grandfather built in
1907," she said. "We lived here with my mother and father at
the time the house was built.

"When I was six years old, in 1910, my family moved to
Vancouver so that we could go to school. My brother Harry and
sister Dorothy and cousins spent every summer on Jedediah

until 1917. My aunt and uncle Morris and Winnie Jelly, Thelma's parents, lived here most of the time.

"My grandparents' boat the *Mary* was our only means of transportation, except two small rowboats. Whoever was on Jedediah had to make the trip with the *Mary*, which took seven hours from Jedediah to Vancouver, to pick up us kids for the summer holidays. My only problem was I was always deathly seasick from the time we passed under the Granville Street Bridge until we reached Jedediah. But summers on Jedediah were wonderful for us."

Al put another piece of heavy bark on the fire and asked if anyone could tell us more about their grandfather, Harry Foote.

Winnie (Foote) Jelly (Morris's wife) and baby Thelma, 1911. Thelma (Jelly) Pohl came to visit Jedediah in 1978 when our neighbour, Cedric Hawkshaw, organized a special get-together for descendants of the pioneers and homesteaders from the area.

"My grandfather, Harry John Foote, was born in London, England in 1859," Alma continued, "and came to Toronto, Ontario with his family at the age of nine. When he moved to Portage la Prairie, he was a licensed auctioneer. Then he started a real estate business. On July 12, 1882 he married Mary Ann Harriet Brooks, one of the twin daughters of Edward Brooks and his wife, pioneers from Stratford, Ontario. In 1890 he moved his family to Vancouver, BC where he operated Foote's Express, with horse and carts. His people met all trains and boats to carry freight to its destination. During this time he organized the first mail collection and parcel service in Vancouver."

"Alma," Thelma interrupted, "is that how he was able to get the government to build docks and wharves on Jedediah and have the mail delivered here for the entire area?"

"Yes, I think that was the case, all right," Alma replied. "Later our grand-

Grandma Mary Foote conducting swimming lessons on Jedediah in the early homesteading years.

father opened another real estate office on Main Street near 7th Avenue, in Vancouver. He was in partnership with the mayor of Vancouver, Walter Owen. This could have been one of his connections in regards to the docks, wharves and mail delivery on Jedediah. Grandfather owned five islands at the time. Jedediah was the largest. I believe Bull, Rabbit, Round and Sheer were the other islands he purchased."

Harry, who had been sitting quietly with Zella and listening to Alma's stories, spoke up. "All was not wine and roses. The family had several tragedies while living on Jedediah. Grandpa's youngest son Lister was tending the sheep in the hills when he slipped over a bank and his gun went off accidentally, wounding him. He tied a bloody handkerchief to his dog and sent him home to get help. The family found him in the hills and gently brought him down and boarded him into their boat. He died on the way to the hospital in Nanaimo.

"Another tragedy was the death of young Gordon Jelly, Thelma's brother. He accidentally fell from the wharf at high tide and was drowned. Remember, Thelma, when you were throwing rocks off a cliff and fell in too? Your mother Winnie jumped in to save you without a thought to the fact that she could not swim either. Everyone had quite a time saving you and your mother. After you were rescued, Grandpa rolled both of you over a large barrel to get the water out of your lungs.

Lister Foote (Harry and Mary Foote's son) and Morris Jelly, 1906. Lister was still a young man when he died. He was tending sheep on the island when his gun went off accidentally and killed him.

"Another brother of yours, Mervyn, died of pneumonia.

"These tragedies took their toll on the family, and Grandpa put the islands up for sale around 1917. He died January 23, 1937. His wife, Mary Foote, passed away in 1953 at the age of eighty-nine."

"I want to tell Al and Mary," Dorothy said, "that three summers ago, my husband Jack and I chartered a launch from Secret Cove on the Sunshine Coast to take us to Jedediah. When we arrived at the island the tide was out and we could not get in Home Bay as we did not have a dinghy. What a great disappointment, because you were living here then. Well, I finally made it back to Jedediah now. I have wanted to return for such a long time. My summers here as a child were pure magic."

Homesteaders on Jedediah, 1916. Seated at front (left to right):
Thelma (Jelly) Pohl, Dorothy (Olmstead) Biggs, Mervyn Jelly (Morris
and Winnie's son, who drowned in 1917), Harry Olmstead, Alma
(Olmstead) Trott. Standing (left to right): Morris Jelly, Mr. Washburn
(a friend from Lasqueti), Winnie Jelly, Mrs. Washburn, Mary Foote,
Lister Foote.

After the historic visit of the Foote family, we received many
gracious letters from Thelma, Dorothy, Alma, Harry and Zella.
The pictures they sent of their family on Jedediah were a treasure to us.

Thelma wrote from Osoyoos, BC soon after our meeting on
Jedediah. "Mary," she wrote, "the swim in the bay with you was
a dream fulfilled. Many years ago, my grandmother, Mary,
taught us children to swim in the same bay. I have no end of
admiration of you folks in the way you have taken to farming,
raising young animals, churning butter, making cheese and all
the myriad of other things you do. I will never forget your
colourful and weedless gardens. I so admire your work, but I am
sure it's pleasurable." She went on to say she hoped we could
meet again, maybe at Osoyoos.

"The enclosed pictures may be of interest to you as they show the dress of the times. I found these recently in an old album my daughter has, there were also pictures of the boat houses and wharf in the front of the house. I believe the government built the docks and wharf."

Other letters followed from the Foote family.

Dorothy (Olmstead) Biggs wrote from Maple Ridge, BC: "I felt so at ease to go anywhere and enjoyed seeing places I spent many childhood hours. To see the house built by my father and grandfather was a joy." She promised to look for her old photographs, and she invited us to visit in Maple Ridge any time.

Alma sent many interesting letters and fine pictures. "These pictures were taken by my Grandma Foote's brother, Will Brook," she wrote in one of her letters. "He had just bought his camera and put in his own darkroom in the basement of our home. He did all his own developing and printing, so some pictures are not as clear as nowadays." Al and I found the pictures to be a treasure. They were clear and they gave a great account of life on Jedediah just after the turn of the century.

A week or two after the Footes' stay, Al and I were hiking along the beach on the northwest side of Jedediah when we saw a large floating building anchored in Anderson Bay on Lasqueti Island.

We had heard from the local people of Lasqueti it was to become a floating hotel for tourists, with accommodations for fishing, and frolicking with a few of the fairer sex. No provisions for washrooms had been made, a noisy generator operated at all hours and small outboard boats pounded the waters of the area.

Residents of Lasqueti were greatly agitated by this intrusion, and there was a suggestion that the enterprise be moved to Deep Bay on Jedediah. We were alarmed. A day or two before the proposed move, we alerted Peter, Esther, Loretta, Darrell on Jedediah, and concerned people living on Texada. Everyone rallied around and a plan was put forth.

To our rescue came a prospector from Texada who was blasting and mining in several areas nearby. The plan was to alert by radiophone all vessels in the area that blasting would take place near Deep Bay on the day the floating hotel proposed to move. The night before the action, the hotel people roped off Deep Bay, blocking access to all other boats, so they would have plenty of room for their operations. Once the hotel was in, no other craft would have room to moor at Deep Bay, which was the only safe moorage for any boat in the area during a storm.

Our prospector arrived at dawn and fastened his dynamite sticks to large pieces of floating bark and driftwood. He radio-phoned to all marine vessels to announce his dynamiting of Deep Bay. We all hiked up a hill to observe the action. The float-ing hotel people had hired a large tugboat to tow the building, and as the tug pulled it along, Esther, who was stationed on the hill behind Deep Bay, blew her horn to alert the prospector it was time to light his fuses.

The prospector was ready. He lit the fuses, and one by one the dynamite sticks blew, with explosions that reverberated back and forth over the water to Lasqueti and back to Jedediah with frightening and deafening reports. As soon as the sound and fury began exploding, the tug turned, swung around the north end of Paul Island and chugged off to the blue yonder, floating hotel in tow.

The people on the hill behind the scene rejoiced. They tum-bled down the hill to meet us on shore and we all revelled in vic-tory. For a few seconds Jedediah had been filled with fire and brimstone, but once again it was a peaceful, pristine place to be.

Indian summers on Jedediah are glorious. Before Big Red could announce the new day, Al and I were awake. The early morning was calm and clear—a fine day to cross over to Lasqueti for our weekly mail.

When we reached Rouse Bay, we anchored the rowboat out in the bay with a long line. We tied another line to shore. Following a path through the seaweed and driftwood, we made our way up to the Phillips family's former home. They had long since moved to Vancouver, and the scene was one of deep desolation. Only an abandoned hull of a house remained. No one greeted us at the half-opened back door.

The lovely gardens were neglected and wild. Yet in the wildness, the scene was serene with towering virgin fir trees reaching to the sky. Beneath the tall trees, verdant ferns and native plants covered the ground. Deer and sheep grazed over all.

We meandered along the path to the main road on Lasqueti. After about a mile of a slight upgrade, we reached our mailbox. Mailboxes on Lasqueti were not your standard government issue, but a variation of containers such as old milk cans, buckets, wooden boxes and backpacks. Local mail delivery people often needed to know who lived with whom at the time of the delivery, as partners changed as often as the weather.

Along with papers, letters and small packages, we found an invitation for an upcoming Greek barbecue. The McFeelys, Kavadas and Collins families were hosting the event on the following Sunday, to introduce the Collinses' future daughter. Peter had proposed marriage to a young lady from the Netherlands.

Al and I were delighted with the invitation. We continued up the main road to see Jean and John at their ranch. The gravel road from our mailbox to the Collins home was a picturesque, rugged piece of landscape. It was barely wide enough for two cars to pass, which was a rare event, as only a few people owned vehicles. Horses, bikes and mare's shank were the more common modes of travel.

After two or three miles of walking, we reached the gate. John Collins was nearby, repairing his sheep fence. When he saw us, he shouted with laughter. "What are you two doing here?" he called.

Al shook John's hand and said, "We are here to thank you for the invitation to your picnic."

"Oh, that," John responded. He took a large handkerchief from his pocket and wiped his entire head and neck. John was a huge fellow, with kindly blue eyes and whitish-grey whiskers that were cropped neatly below his chin. "Come on in," he said, "and have a chitchat with Jean and me. I have a new batch of wine I'd like you to try."

Jean met us by their large, screened back porch and greeted us in her Texas drawl. "Come on in, y'all, and rest a bit. You look a frightful tuckered out."

Jean was a small lady with short cropped grey hair and twinkling eyes that sparkled with vitality. Both John and Jean were retired schoolteachers and librarians who had lived in the Seattle area. Before they retired, they had gone in search of secluded country farmland. They purchased this large, old homestead on Lasqueti and diligently worked the land and buildings. The Collins spread was a vital, thriving farm where everyone was warmly welcomed.

Their sons Sam and Peter were fine young men. They spent their summers on Lasqueti and attended college in the States during the winter months. As the

Al Palmer, 1989.

years passed, they became very successful men.

John poured Al, Jean and me a glass of lovely red wine. Al made a toast. "Here's to all islanders. May they always prosper in health and happiness." Our glasses clinked and Jean offered everyone cheese and biscuits. Both John and Jean were excellent gourmet chefs and gracious hosts. We enjoyed many a fine dining experience at their island home.

The Collinses also offered a port in a storm. In winter, when our boat could not return to Jedediah due to stormy weather, we found not only refuge but great fun staying a day or two with the Collins family.

Our other Lasqueti stormbound or "cabin fever" friends were the Miller family. Dave and Aileen had immigrated from Scotland and spent a few years in the real estate trade in northern British Columbia. From this business they were able to seek their rewards on Lasqueti, and during the 1960s that is where they found their Shangri-La. Dave and Aileen raised three sons and two daughters on Lasqueti and made a beautiful home and garden on the west side of the island, looking across the water toward Vancouver Island.

Al and I spent many a rollicking stormbound time at the Millers'. The *Manchester Guardian* was Dave's paper and Al was a convert to *The Globe and Mail*. Discourses on the right and the left were often undertaken in good spirits, well into a winter's night.

The Greek barbecue at the Collins home that Sunday was a gourmet's delight. Authentic Greek dishes were offered, with local lamb prepared to perfection with fresh herbs. Home-brewed wines and beers lulled us all into complete submission to the food, company and surroundings. The festivities extended from the afternoon well into the night. Everyone was overjoyed to meet Peter's intended, a lovely girl from the Netherlands. I believe she was pretty overwhelmed by so many islanders. Most islanders are quite individualistic in manners, and many have peculiar traits. But they are extremely loyal to each other and most maintain a contented and peaceful countenance.

Many neighbours of Jean and John's attended the event. One of them was Ruby Nichols, a longtime friend from the early days of my arrival on Jedediah. Ruby was happily married to Eric, a son of pioneers of Lasqueti. Eric was the road foreman on Lasqueti and kept a fine open road. Ruby was a very attractive lady, active in the local PTA. They had a son, Christopher. At the picnic Ruby and I had a grand time remembering our adventures together on the island in the early 1950s.

Betty and Ed Darwin were also enjoying the gathering. Betty was a courageous, vital woman, very athletic and active in the community. However, the last few years had taken a toll on her health. She was waging a war with arthritis and had become blind. Yet even these conditions did not prevent her from taking part in every phase of life. She had an Olympic-sized swimming pool at her home on Lasqueti and she logged one hundred laps per day. Ed was a devoted husband and father to their six children. He was also a skilled brewmaster and to everyone's approval, he brought his special ale to the barbecue.

Mary and Craig McFeely lived near the Collinses. They had bought their property from Jean and John a few years earlier and were great neighbours. Gloria and Alex Kavadas, the third set of hosts, lived high on a bluff near the Miller home. They had been bewitched by Lasqueti in the early 1960s. Now they were retired, although Alex was a renowned physicist who still lectured at many universities around the world. Gloria and Alex gave much to the community of Lasqueti.

As dusk crept in and we reminisced about past gatherings on the islands, John said, "We really miss Rosa at these parties. Now there was a girl that could eat and she didn't mind a bit of brew, either." Rosa, her husband Karl, and son Karl had come to Lasqueti from Germany. Karl Sr. was an actor and lithographer in Germany and Rosa was a nurse trained in Europe. She was also an avid outdoorsperson, capable of carpentry and gardening. Karl passed away in 1966, and Rosa had lived on for many years.

"I remember, Mary," said Jean, "you wrote a piece in a Seattle paper about Rosa's funeral. I clipped it out." She set her dessert tray down and went into the house for the article.

Rosa was big and beautiful. Now she is gone. Nearly eight decades of pioneering gave her great strength and fortitude.

It seems unbelievable such a vibrant spirit is no more. When Rosa took ill, a helicopter landed in the school grounds on Lasqueti Island, BC and took Rosa away to the hospital.

Some say she was suffering from celebrating Christmas with too many gastronomic delights. Happiness to Rosa was a full larder, a brewing crock and lively companions. Each time she heard footsteps on her back porch, there was a scurrying in the pantry for a few aged bottles of home brew. This brew was from a special secret recipe from her native Germany.

Homemade cheese, bread and salty smoked salmon were added to the table. Fascinating tales followed as the brew and food disappeared. Rosa, after forty years on Lasqueti, was overflowing in yarns of yesterday.

Youngsters barely able to climb her back steps were spellbound by her stories. Often they chided her that she was fat and old. Spirited Rosa would toss her head back and roar with laughter until tears washed her full, round cheeks. When the young ones were ready to leave, they were given a pat and a fresh cookie just out of the old wood stove oven.

Whenever we passed her cottage along the old dirt road on the island, we saw Rosa kneeling down tending her garden.

Each spring, we were refreshed in her world of daffodils, tulips, trilliums, violets and forget-me-nots. Overhead the hummingbirds were visiting the blossoms of the native arbutus trees. Spring blossoms smothered her flowing wild currant, cherry and plum trees.

Fruit trees and berry patches rewarded her each summer and fall. All was stored, canned or, as she would say, "bottled" for the winter.

When autumn was the scene, Rosa's garden was brilliant. Only deep winter found it dreary.

Who would take care of her garden now that she was gone? News of her passing reached the island folks quickly, by radiophone from the hospital in Nanaimo. Everyone was alerted and saddened. Rosa was dead.

The ferry captain, Ian Cole, and his deckhand Sandy Gillespie painted the interior of the small, passenger vessel a lively yellow to bring Rosa home.

According to her wishes, a simple ceremony was to be held on the island. Only her neighbours and friends were to stand and speak over her open grave.

Island neighbours and friends prepared her place in the community graveyard. The burial site is in a wooded area. A rugged cedar fence is useful in restricting ranging cattle, sheep, deer and goats. Ancient wrought-iron or cedar picket fences box in a few of the older graves. Headstones fashioned from local stone or marble crosses mark many graves. Some markers are made of a chain-saw handle or a rusty boat anchor. A few graves are planted with native trees, shrubs and spring-flowing bulbs, primroses or pansies. Ferns grow over all.

As the ferry boat slowly made its way to the dock, islanders stood by in the morning sunlight, waiting for Rosa.

All manner of dress was worn. Some mourners were noticeably uncomfortable in shiny blue serge suits, with small bow ties. Others were in freshly washed jeans and jackets. Women were admired in their "going to town best."

A few young girls wore "granny dresses" and kerchiefs. Wiggly babies were strapped to their mothers' and fathers' backs. Straight, tall young men with shaggy hair and bristle beards were sombre. A few wore hunting knives in their leather belts.

School was dismissed for this day. A score of youngsters mingled among the others, bright and shiny in their best. Rosa would want them waiting at the dockside too. One young fellow muttered, "Remember last summer, when Rosa came down to the dock, dove into the water and swam clear out to the raft?"

The gathering was silent as the casket was carefully removed from the ferry. It was lifted by six husky men into a station wagon.

The sun was shining for Rosa, as she was driven along the narrow gravel road.

A few folks were waiting beside the open grave. It was dark, deep and boarded with cedar planks on the sides. Two thickly braided ropes were waiting to lower the casket. On each side were huge humps of newly dug earth. Shovels and two picks were thrust into the humps.

As Rosa was gently lowered into her carefully dug

grave, silent tears were shed. Everyone was standing in a large semicircle around the grave. Johnny Osland gave an impressive eulogy in honour of Rosa. He had been a friend of Rosa and Karl Shumach since the 1940s.

Johnny accepted the responsibility of maintaining the cemetery and conducting the funerals on Lasqueti Island.

All heads were bowed when the tribute to Rosa was finished. Shovels were taken in hand, first by the youngest of the island. They placed the earth slowly and carefully around the sides of Rosa's casket. The young ones were replaced by teen-agers. Then all took turns in blanketing the grave. A single red rose was added before the last shovel was laid down.

Bouquets and sprays of flowers were arranged over the mound. Sprigs of spring blossoms from cherry, plum and dogwood were tied in bunches and fastened with brightly coloured yarn. Green and red salal and mahonia leaves were fashioned into a wreath and placed among the others.

A rugged cross was formed of native daffodils from Jedediah. Floral arrangements of roses, carnations and chrysanthemums from town were also lovingly placed on Rosa's grave.

Each mourner took a few steps forward in reverence, then slowly made his way to the open gate of the cemetery. One by one the islanders departed, closing the creaky hinge of the cemetery gate.

After Jean read the account of Rosa's funeral, the group was silent. Betty Darwin broke the stillness by lifting her glass and giving a toast to Rosa.

A few folks took their leave. Many stayed on to enjoy more

food and drink. Soon Al and I found our way into the Millers' truck and were whisked off to their home for the night. Not too early the following day, we all arose to the smell of bacon sizzling. Scotch scones, tea and ranch eggs gave us the needed nourishment to continue home to Jedediah.

Our late summers on Jedediah were filled with daily chores. We gathered wood, storing and stacking it for year-round use. Al had an old wooden wagon and an ancient Case tractor that he used for hauling sections of fallen logs to the wood storage shed. Many of our guests and visitors pitched in to help, and most enjoyed riding the wagon and driving the tractor, especially the teenagers.

Another chore our grandchildren enjoyed was the bottling of our wine, root beer, ginger beer and alcoholic beer. They weren't as fond of churning butter, which we did every few days. The process was slow and arm-tiring, and the youngsters grew impatient. Yet they found it fascinating to watch the thick cream gradually turn into golden bubbles of butter.

By late summer Al's vegetable garden was overflowing with crops to be stored in jars or dried. Flower gardens were blazing in colour now, and needed extra watering and cutting back. This was the time to take a few for dried flowers to cheer the winter. Natural hay was cut and stored in the barn, and extra hay and grain were brought in by boat while the weather was cooperative. Each year the Mann boys brought us our winter's supply of gas, kerosene, hay and grain. This expedition was combined with an annual picnic on Jedediah.

The 1981 picnic was very special. It was to celebrate twenty years of the Mann family living on Jedediah, where they had moved from De Courcy Island in 1961.

Ron and Hetty Mann brought two large fish boats, the *Osprey* and the *Adonis*, filled with relatives and friends. Merl skippered the *Adonis* and Ron the *Osprey*. Wesley captained the

Our summer picnic in the pasture on Jedediah, 1981. We always looked forward to this event, when family and friends came from all over the area to eat, drink, swim, play ball, sing songs, tell stories and remember absent friends.

Lasqueti Gambler, a fishing vessel built and owned by the Forbes and Millicheap fishing company. Members of the Mann and Ryan family plus other friends and relatives spilled overboard from all of the fish boats.

Aboard the *Osprey*, Ron and Hetty Mann's boat, on the occasion of our annual summer picnic at Jedediah, 1980. This vessel transported Al and me and our belongings to Nanoose when we moved away from Jedediah.

When they arrived early in the morning, the tide was out in Home Bay. They anchored the boats out in the deep water of the channel and used various Zodiacs and hurricane crafts to ferry people and supplies from the fish boats to shore. These small craft could navigate in only a few inches of water during the incoming tide.

The first boatload were small folks. Some were deathly frightened and seasick and others were filled with hyper energy. The teenagers were quickly up from the shore to the kitchen, to sample the doughnuts I was making for the crew. The youngsters helped deep-fry the doughnuts and roll them in icing sugar and melted chocolate. Only a few morsels remained when the main crew arrived.

Quickly the orchard and fields were covered in brightly coloured tents. Portable propane stoves were lit and the coffee was on. The sheep and cows scattered, but watched the invasion from a distance. Will the horse nosed into everything, being a pest. The older children reached up into the apple trees for treats to give to Will. He was ecstatic with the apples and the attention. Later in the afternoon, all the young ones and a few of the adults had rides on Will. He was careful of the little ones, but would give the older folks a run for their money. Eventually the cows and sheep became curious, enough to venture up to the standing tents and lean on them, breaking some down. A few cows pushed into

A row of Ryan and Mann youngsters ready to head out on the water, 1989.

the openings of the tents for a closer look. One old ram sheep ran back and forth, butting people's behinds.

While the adults were busy setting up camp, the little ones explored the area. As two large pet turkeys strutted about, the children put their tiny hats and coats on the turkeys, with squeals of laughter. Finally one of the turkeys got fed up with the attention, put up his two feet and gave little Sheryl Mann a big push down to the ground. The game was over. Tears and howls followed.

These turkeys were very active and followed us everywhere. When we were hiking in the woods and they had difficulty keeping up with us or climbing over logs and brush, they protested with gobbling noises until we helped them or waited for them to catch up.

A baseball diamond had been marked off out in one of the fields, and the games ran all afternoon. Those Ryan gals could sure pitch a mean ball, but the Mann gals could run and hit. So the games were fair and shared. Everyone who could catch, throw or run played ball.

Other folks found water sports more to their liking. Little ones followed the tide in over the warm sand and hunted for special shells, sand dollars, starfish and other creatures. Teenagers water-skied or rode boards towed behind speedboats driven by Vern, Ron, Alfie and Dan. Sidney Ryan took some of the young ones out in the main channel to fish. The Ryan girls were great swimmers.

Al chugging off to our picnic grounds with a load of kids on a hay wagon.

When the tide was high in the bay, the skippers all brought the fish boats into shore and unloaded hay, grain, kerosene, gas and other supplies we might need during the long winters on Jedediah. While everyone was enjoying the fun, Shirley Mann, Hetty and her mother Frances were busy preparing food for the crowd. Helen Ryan and I kept the home stove going with extra rations on hand. The young fellows built a large outdoor firepit and placed a heavy iron grill over it for cooking and barbecuing. In early morning the older campers crawled out of their tents and started the fire in the outdoor pit and propane stoves. One by one the camp was invaded by hungry youngsters ready for breakfast.

The elderly folk stayed in our farmhouse. We kept the kitchen range going for comfort and cooking, and campers stopped in for an extra cup of coffee or a pancake or two while waiting for the outdoor kitchen to get going full swing. After breakfast, guests took long hikes over the island or started up a baseball game or helped Al with the outdoor chores. Poor old Rosie the cow had her milk spigots squeezed and pulled endlessly in an attempt to get fresh milk. She was patient and let them all try.

The days of the annual picnics were too short. Al and I looked forward to having the Ryan and Mann families back with us on Jedediah. By this time one of our old friends, Art Ryan, was missing from our gatherings. He had gone fishing and was drowned near Lasqueti. Helen and her children continued to live on Lasqueti for many years after Art's death. He was a part of the BC coast and is greatly missed by us all.

Several days after the picnic, Al was cutting the front lawn with an old manual lawn mower when he noticed a large sailboat drifting into Home Bay. The tide was going out rapidly, so he yelled down to the skipper that he should anchor out of the bay until high tide. But he was too late. The sailboat was grounded

Enjoying each other's company, 1980s. Left to right: Bill Cox, Margaret Boyer, Jim Dougan, me, Al and Sam Lamont.

and lay on its side. Al ran down to the beach. "Have you shut all your portholes, hatches and any other openings?" he asked.

"No," was the answer. Al and the skipper quickly fastened any openings that might fill with seawater when the tide rushed back in.

The fellow introduced himself as John, and asked Al if he could come on shore for a visit. Al welcomed him, but said John had better help him get some planks and bolster up the hull of the boat so that it would be upright when the tide began to come back in. The two men found some sturdy planks by the barn and braced the boat upright. Then they came into the kitchen for a cup of coffee while they awaited the fate of the sailboat. "I go by Jedediah often," John told us, "but have never sailed into this bay. I have been taking land surveyors over to the south end of Texada all this summer. I dropped off three men this morning and jokingly told them that I hadn't been paid for the last three trips and would leave them there if their boss didn't come through with the money soon. Now this would be a can of worms if I don't return, or am late in picking them up."

Al asked, "Have they a radiophone with them?"

"No, one of the fellows left the phone at home."

"Well then, they'll just have to wait until the tide comes in, and hope the boat uprights and floats."

"Oh my God, don't think like that," said John. "I have no insurance on the boat, and my wife thinks I took out insurance. She will give me billy hell if I lose the boat, as our house is mortgaged with it."

John lit up one cigarette after another and nervously paced up and down the kitchen, until Al finally suggested they go back down to the beach and double-check the boat.

Inch by inch, the tidewater lapped the keel of the boat. The tide rose more swiftly as the two men watched the water creep up the hull. The boat creaked and lifted, the planks held it upright, and finally all was well. The boat was freely floating again. John and his sailboat glided out of the bay, into the dusk. We never heard whether the surveyors panicked when darkness fell and they were left with no transportation back to civilization. We are sure they gave their boss the word to pay up. Also, we can be certain John has insurance on his sailboat now.

At harvest time, the cherry trees in the orchard are ablaze in vermilion and gold. Each autumn we had the privilege of judging the fall fair on Lasqueti, and observing the results of all the efforts the locals put into gardening, harvesting, canning and preserving their produce. Categories of entries ranged from homemade beer and wine, to baked goods, needlework and special children's crafts. Al and I judged the flower arranging and fruits and vegetables. We took our judging task seriously and enjoyed it. Each year we were more impressed with the displays. The crafts and art work done by the youngsters were creative and impressive.

The Lasqueti Island fall fair, 1989. For many years Al and I were honoured to serve as judges of fruits, vegetables and flower arranging, and we loved seeing the good work of our Lasqueti friends and neighbours on display.

Music is provided by local musicians. The sounds of guitars, drums, horns and fiddles blend in lively tunes. Minstrels wander about the crowds displaying their talents and creating a festive, spirited atmosphere. In the afternoon, a salmon barbecue is held, complete with homemade cider, beer and wine, along with sweets for dessert.

Early in the day, we judge the produce behind closed doors. After the blue, red and white ribbons are placed on the winning items, the doors are open to all to check out the results. Murmurs ripple through the crowd as people lean over the displays, ponder our decisions and decide whether they agree with our choices. We stand nearby and take in their responses and deliberations, all offered in a friendly manner.

The day is also spent visiting folks and catching up on the news of Lasqueti. Plans for the next fall fair are discussed and suggestions for improvements are made. As the day dwindles down, young children become overtired and irritable, and grumpy golden-agers straggle homeward. Al and I are given a ride to Squitty Bay, where our boat is moored. Before the autumn sky is darkened, we are home again on Jedediah.

After the 1981 fall fair, we got home to find a thirty-two-foot cabin cruiser anchored in Home Bay. It bore a licence plate from Washington state and two marine flags, one of Canada and the other of the States. Standing near the stern of the boat was Al's brother Bob, his longtime chum Blaine Freer, and Blaine's wife Sar-Ann. Al yelled over to their boat, "Where did you come from, and how long have you been in the bay?"

Carolin and Brent Campbell, the son of Lennis Mann Campbell, take a ride on Will, early 1980s.

"Why don't you stay home and wait for your loving brother?" Bob yelled back.

"I would have if I knew you were on your way," was Al's reply. "You always were one for surprises."

Al took Sar-Ann onto our boat and took us "girls" into shore. Then the three men tied the boats together and anchored them securely. We all crept into the sack soon after reaching the house.

One by one we all found coffee perking on the cook stove the next morning. Al was out in the barn milking Rosie before Sar-Ann or I got down to the kitchen. It was great fun having those three. Our days were spent fishing, hiking, exploring the island and just enjoying each other. Evenings were times for reminiscing about the adventures and experiences we had had together, on this visit and in the past.

Blaine was the outdoor editor of the *Seattle Post-Intelligencer*. After his visit with us he wrote the following account of his stay on Jedediah:

The house at Home Bay, 1983.

You can find Jedediah Island on a chart of the Strait of Georgia, lying just inside the southern tips of huge Texada Island and its somewhat smaller neighbor to the west, Lasqueti Island. Other than a float plane, the only way to visit them is by boat. Owning and living year-round on an small island would be paradise only for those who, by training and temperament, enjoy that sort of life.

Al is a graduate fisheries biologist from the University of Washington. He was employed by the UW as a research biologist, and spent many summers in Alaska doing salmon research. I have known him since he was born.

Mary was garden editor for the *Seattle Post-Intelligencer*, then the *Seattle Times*, and now writes for the *Arboretum Bulletin*, published by the UW press.

So, what kind of a temperament does it take? One might suppose they would tend to be reclusive. In fact they are the exact opposite, being just about the most extroverted people you'll ever see or hear.

Al and I tending the garden, 1986.

Now how much time do they spend fishing? Very little. The reason may be found in that their vegetable garden is now growing, or has grown, just about every kind of vegetable you can name, including such unlikely experiments as soybeans, peanuts, cotton and lemon trees in their sunroom.

They have many fruit trees, including apples, pears, plums and cherries, plus some nectarine, peach and apricot trees that they are growing for an experimental station in Ontario, Canada. Oh yes, eucalyptus, guavas and figs are grown along with a huge selection of shrubs and flowers. They send to Kew

Al's vegetable garden, 1982. Few visitors left Jedediah without a souvenir of some fresh local produce.

Gardens in England for seeds of many types of trees, shrubs and other plants.

Add to this chickens, geese, ducks and guinea hens, a milk cow, a herd bull, a dozen or more beef cattle, over 100 head of sheep, Will the horse, two dogs and a cat.

Yes, Al and Mary are so busy with their flowers, veggies and livestock, they don't have much time left for fishing. But somehow it's hard to feel sorry for them. We all had a grand time on the private paradise of the Palmers'.

For Al and me, the seasons passed too rapidly. At the end of twenty years, we were finding our spirits were willing, but the energy was winding down. We had retired to Jedediah when we were fifty years old, now we were both looking at seventy years of age.

We agonized with the knowledge that we would have to

Taking a break, 1988. Left to right: Carolin, Andy, Evan, me, Sally, Roger and a buddy.

The house at Home Bay getting a new sunroom, 1991.

leave Jedediah in the near future. Operating a productive farm, keeping a ten-cord woodpile going, tending orchards and gardens plus maintaining a large seaworthy boat—it was beginning to be beyond us. Many times we had hired help, but most found the isolation foreboding after a short time. Without the farm status, the land taxes on Jedediah would rise astronomically. It was time to make the change. We would have to leave Jedediah.

One grey, dreary day in 1992, the *Osprey* anchored in Home Bay with Ron and Hetty Mann aboard. During their visit, they announced they would be back next week with two or three boats and move us to their farm near Nanoose, BC.

The following week was an extremely difficult time for us. Leaving Jedediah was like parting with our souls. Now it was necessary for us to be in closer contact with people who would negotiate ways of leaving Jedediah in trust. Al and I wanted to explore ways in which we could preserve Jedediah in its pristine condition in perpetuity, without sacrificing its land, native plants, timber, beaches and other unique features.

Ron, Dan, Vern and Wes Mann plus their wives and girl-friends all helped us move our belongings from Jedediah to the farm at Nanoose. It was a difficult exercise. Even an old upright piano rode the salty waves, and my grandmother's Havilland china and china cabinet had a bumpy return trip. Thanks to all the willing hands, we were able to settle in at Ron and Hetty's farm. The move was traumatic, but we felt the caring and warmth of the Mann family immediately, and began to adjust to our new life.

We made a few trips back to Jedediah to bring the cattle, sheep and poultry to the farm. Will, the old horse, was content to remain on the island. To move him to the city would have been terrifying for him. A young boatbuilder who stayed on at the north end of Jedediah agreed to care for Will.

It wasn't long before Al and I began making trips to Vancouver to talk to federal government people about the possibility of their purchasing Jedediah for a park. They were willing to listen and assured us they were interested in the proposal. But the endless rules, regulations, policies and guidelines made the project seem hopeless.

In despair, we offered the island for sale through a real estate agent, with the stipulation it would remain a park forever. A Toronto group of investors offered us $7.9 million, and another offer from Dallas, Texas was well over the mark. Then the Nature Conservancy of Canada, a Toronto-based charitable organization, began to negotiate with us. Bill Merilees, a local naturalist and co-author of *Trees, Shrubs, and Flowers to Know in British Columbia and Washington*, worked for a year or two with us and the Nature Conservancy to formulate an agreement. Bill was tireless in his efforts to facilitate the purchase. He gave tremendous support to saving Jedediah for a park.

At one point, when negotiations came to a standstill, our friend Rosalind Hildred from Bull Island wrote many letters to different news media and government agencies urging them to purchase Jedediah for a park. Pete McMartin of the *Vancouver Sun* wrote a great story describing the plight of Jedediah. It was published along with a map and pictures.

This timely article began a chain reaction. The evening the article appeared, we received a phone call from Bruce Culver, brother of Dan Culver, one of the most accomplished wilderness adventurers of the world. He was a dedicated environmentalist who had put great effort into saving the Tatshenshini River, the Khutzeymateen Valley, Clayoquot Sound and Robson Bight, in BC. He and Jim Haberl were the first Canadians to reach summit K2, the world's highest peak, in 1993. On July 7, 1993, Dan fell to his death while climbing down the summit of K2. Bruce Culver told us that Dan had specified in his will that part of his

Al and friends admire the new memorial to Dan Culver, 1995. Culver was a BC mountaineer and environmentalist whose estate made it possible to designate Jedediah as a provincial marine park.

estate be used to preserve a wilderness area on the BC coast. This gave us new hope, and the incentive to contact the provincial government about the purchase. News of the Culver family's generous donation inspired an outpouring of enthusiasm and generosity from many individuals and organizations.

In December 1994, Environment, Lands and Parks Minister Moe Sihota announced that the province was in the process of purchasing Jedediah Island for $4.2 million—a price that was substantially below market value. The province had agreed to pay $2.6 million, the Culver estate donated $1.1, and further commitments were made by the Friends of Jedediah, the Marine Parks Forever Society, The Nature Trust of BC, Mountain Equipment Co-op, Marine Trades Association and Canada Trust.

Other organizations and corporations were approached, the media were asked to do stories on Jedediah to raise awareness, booths were set up at the Vancouver and Victoria boat shows,

Sunset on Home Bay, a sight Al and I will always remember.

and a benefit concert featuring Shari Ulrich was held in Victoria. Many individuals sent donations, and community and corporate gifts made up the shortfall.

The government of BC announced the completion of the purchase of Jedediah Island on March 6, 1995. Jedediah is now a Class A provincial park, the highest level of provincial land protection in the Park Act.

For Al and me, being part of Jedediah's designation as a park was a bittersweet experience. We were sad to leave Jedediah, our literal and spiritual home for many years and a way of life for us. But we are happy in the knowledge that generations of people will benefit and find idyllic refuge in Jedediah forever.

Afterword

Jedediah Island is a remarkable place, which was recognized by Mary and Al Palmer. Through their vision and patience, they presented the government of British Columbia with the opportunity to protect this island paradise for the people of British Columbia. The park was made a reality through the generosity of Mary and Al Palmer, the fundraising efforts of the Friends of Jedediah, a generous gift from the Dan Culver estate, and contributions from hundreds of generous individuals, groups and corporations.

On March 6, 1995, Jedediah Island was protected under the Park Act so that future generations may be able to enjoy the solitude and natural beauty of the island. In keeping with the spirit that led to the protection of this special island, BC Parks will continue to work co-operatively with the Palmers, and people of British Columbia, to ensure that the natural, heritage and recreational values—for which Jedediah is locally loved—continue for future generations to enjoy and treasure as much as we do.

Hon. Cathy McGregor
Minister of Environment, Lands and Parks
Victoria, BC
March 1998